Write to the Point!

Kim Henderson

Addison-Wesley Publishing Company

Reading, Massachusetts • Menlo Park, California • New York
Don Mills, Ontario • Wokingham, England • Amsterdam • Bonn
Sydney • Singapore • Tokyo • Madrid • San Juan

A Publication of the World Language Division

Editorial: Kathleen Sands Boehmer and Karen Doyle

Production/Manufacturing: James W. Gibbons

Design: PC & F, Inc.

Cover Design: Prentice Crosier

Illustrations: Kim Henderson pp. 18, 45, 46, 49, 65, 66, 100, 166; Barbara Lübberger pp. 88, 103, 117, 118, 120, 126; PC & F, Inc. pp. 11, 19, 32, 33, 52, 53, 113, 159

Photo Acknowledgments: Addison-Wesley p. 57 (a); Center for History of Physics p. 1; Christopher Columbus High School, Bronx, NY p. 135; Charlotte Dihoff p. 99 (a); Augustin Estrada p. 99 (e); Diane Fox p. 136; Johan Hagemeyer, Bancroft Library p. 5; Kim Henderson pp. 38, 57, 58, 61, 62, 67, 68, 108, 139, 156, 163, 164, 165; Japan Airlines p. 155; Reginald McGovern p. 99 (c); NASA p. 77; New York Convention and Visitors Bureau p. 77; Salem High School, New Hampshire pp. 27, 99 (a) & (d); Tennessee Tourist Development p. 17; WCVB TV p. 99 (f); Guenther Zuern p. 37

Library of Congress Cataloging-in-Publication Data

Henderson, Kim.
   Write to the Point! / Kim Henderson.
      p.   cm.
   Includes index.
   ISBN 0-201-50353-0
   1. English language--Textbooks for foreign speakers. 2. English language--Rhetoric. 3. College readers. I. Title. II. Title: Reading and writing for beginning/intermediate students.
PE1128.H426 1990
808'.0427--dc20

ISBN 0-201-50353-0

10-CRS-97 96 95 94

CONTENTS

INTRODUCTION

Approach

This is a beginning/intermediate writing textbook and workbook for English as a Second Language students who are preparing for entry into American universities. This text is intended for an intensive ESL program which offers basic skills courses (reading, writing, grammar, listening, speaking) and courses in English for academic purposes. Although the primary goal of this text is to improve writing skills, it integrates reading, speaking, grammar and writing activities.

The connection between reading and writing is an important focus in this text. When students enter American universities, much of the required writing is in response to reading textbooks, periodicals, reference books, research materials, etc. The philosophy behind this text is that ESL students should begin making the reading-writing connection as soon as possible. Thus, readings are not used only as rhetorical and grammatical models but as resources for information and ideas.

This text attempts to put into practice H.G. Widdowson's ideas on learner participation and the strategy of "gradual approximation." This strategy offers students a reading-writing process: pre-reading and reading activities are followed by comprehension and writing activities that allow the students to work with the reading in several ways. Through this process, which moves from sentence level work to summary work and ultimately to student generated discourse in speaking and writing, students gradually absorb both the ideas and the structure of passages to a point where they are ready to communicate their own ideas. The key factor in such an approach is, of course, engaging students' interest. They must care about what they read, have problems to solve, and have relevant reasons to use English in order to see it not as patterns, but as a tool to be used as they use their native languages: to describe, to explain, to argue, to speculate, to tell stories.

Organization

Each chapter of the text contains two readings. The first reading has an academic, informational theme. With the first reading, gradual approximation activities are carefully sequenced:

1. There is a pre-reading activity with a picture, chart or graph. Students use the picture, chart or graph to do oral or written sentence level work with the ideas, vocabulary and grammar of the reading before they have seen the reading. By chapter 3, students are able to approximate a summary of the reading or a part of the reading before they have done the reading.

2. The reading is followed by an Interpretation Check which includes vocabulary recognition and main ideas and details. Grammar points are also reviewed within a comprehension exercise framework.

3. Following the Interpretation Check, grammar points are practiced in a series of written exercises based on the reading. These transformation, completion and matching exercises require the student to consider the function of grammar before form since they must understand the ideas, vocabulary and grammar of the reading in order to do the written exercises.

4. In the final step of this sequence, the student writes a one or two paragraph summary of the reading using the material in the Interpretation Check and the written exercises. In the beginning chapters, the student is carefully guided toward this step. In the final chapters, the student is given more independence. In addition, the final chapters include a higher level step; summaries are rewritten or expanded using rhetorical transformation.

The second reading contains some but not all elements of the gradual approximation process. Each reading begins with a pre-reading activity and is followed by an Interpretation Check, but the written exercises do not guide the student to summary writing. Instead, more emphasis is placed on practicing other writing skills such as sentence combining, punctuation, and writing topic sentences. The second readings are student compositions and are meant to provide more personal reading and to expand on the grammar and vocabulary of the first reading. These readings are also something of a model for students when they think about their own compositions.

Each reading and writing section in a chapter is followed by a "Let's Talk" activity. This activity provides a communicative task: usually a problem solving or information gap task, which requires students to recycle grammar and vocabulary in somewhat different contexts. Students are then asked to write paragraphs based on the previous speaking activity.

Each chapter concludes with discussion questions and pre-writing activities to help the student in the composition process. The pre-writing activities include brainstorming, listing, outlining, clustering, and drawing a picture. Two or three drafts are suggested for each composition. Recommendations for revision include reader-based comments on the first draft and grammar and mechanics correction of the second draft.

A pre/post grammar test is included in the Appendices. When students begin using this text, they are expected to be familiar with, but not masters of, the grammar covered in the text: parts of speech; past, present and future tenses and past and present continuous tenses; imperatives; comparative and superlative adjectives; count and non count nouns and quantifiers; prepositions of place and time; sentence connectors: *and, but, because, so, when, after, before, if.*

To the Teacher

A chapter might be taught as follows: You present the pre-reading activity in class using as many visual aids and eliciting as much vocabulary and free discussion as possible. Students can do reading, Interpretation Check and grammar exercises in class or as homework. However, you should do summary activities in class since these are often difficult for students. When reviewing readings or exercises, overhead projector materials are especially helpful to beginning students. Particularly with exercises that have a discourse element: cloze passages, main idea spotting, and sequencing sentences in paragraph writing, students will be able to understand more quickly if you can point things out on a screen.

The nine chapters of the text are sequenced in degree of difficulty. However, the first chapter has longer and more difficult readings than the other beginning chapters, and it has a quick introduction to past, present and future tense. The reason for the difficulty of this chapter is to help you determine student abilities early in the term. If a student has no trouble with the first reading or with using the three basic tenses in writing, this student may need to move up a level. The first chapter also has important information on parts of speech and sentence structure. Students will need to know the terminology of sentence structure in order to conference with you on writing problems. The final chapter is essentially a review chapter intended to give the student some experience in synthesizing the rhetorical forms presented in the text.

The "Let's Talk" activities need careful introduction, especially the first few times students do them. Since most talking activities require students to use grammar covered in the chapter, particularly question forms, it is helpful to do a brief review of that grammar before students begin talking. Also, some vocabulary may need explanation before students begin. It is important to monitor students during this activity to see that they understand and can do the activity correctly. It is also important to be available for questions on grammar, vocabulary and pronunciation. When students finish talking, you should review the activity as a class to reinforce correct forms and pronunciation.

The pre-writing and revision activities should be adapted according to the level of the class. These activities will be more successful with a more intermediate group. Thinking about main ideas and organization before writing can be very difficult for a beginning student. Also, beginning students aren't likely to be able to do peer revision. Beginning students may need more help or more structure than the text suggests. In general, it would appear that whether a student is beginning or advanced, personal conferences with you do much more toward helping the student with writing than written comments. Therefore, the guidelines for reader based and grammar based written comments and the revision checklist are meant to be used at your discretion. One final suggestion is that you keep everything a student writes in one folder: all paragraphs, summaries, pre-writing, 1st and 2nd drafts and compositions so that both you and the student can note special recurring writing problems, and more importantly, student progress.

Acknowledgments

I'd like to thank Dr. James Nattinger of Portland State University for his excellent and inspiring teaching of applied linguistics. First he revealed the theory. Then he challenged us to use it.

I would also like to thank Dr. Virginia Samuda for her practical support and advice and for guiding me to Addison-Wesley.

1 Biography

A biography is a story of a person's life. In this chapter, we will look at the biography of a famous person, Albert Einstein, and a biography that someone wrote about himself.

THE LIFE OF ALBERT EINSTEIN

Exercise A

Discuss the time line below. Make sentences about the life of Albert Einstein.

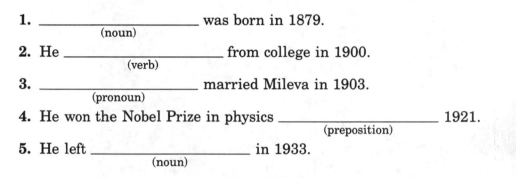

was born	graduated	married Mileva	published "Theory of Relativity"	won Nobel Prize	left Germany	died
1879	1900	1903	1905	1921	1933	1955

Exercise B

Use the words in the time line to complete the sentences below.

1. _____ was born in 1879.
   (noun)

2. He _____ from college in 1900.
   (verb)

3. _____ married Mileva in 1903.
   (pronoun)

4. He won the Nobel Prize in physics _____ 1921.
   (preposition)

5. He left _____ in 1933.
   (noun)

Parts of Speech

When we talk about English grammar, it is helpful to talk about parts of speech. Each word in an English sentence can be considered a part of speech. Here is a simple explanation of the main parts of speech:

noun: A noun is a person, place, or a thing. (man, Japan, tree)

pronoun: A pronoun is used like a noun. There are subject, object, and possessive pronouns.
subject pronouns: I, you, he, she, it, we, you, they
object pronouns: me, you, him, her, it, us, you, them
possessive pronouns: mine, yours, his, hers, its, ours, yours, theirs

verb: A verb shows action (run, sit, eat), or being (is, are, am)
Verbs have different tenses to show time. In this book, we will use present, present continuous, past, past continuous, and future verb tenses.

adjective: An adjective describes a noun. (beautiful, tall, large)
An adjective is often before a noun.

    Example: That is a *beautiful* tree.

adverb: An adverb modifies verbs, adjectives or other adverbs and is in different places in a sentence. Adverbs often describe how often, or in what way a verb action happens.

    Example: The man runs *quickly.*

preposition: A preposition often tells *when* (on Friday) or *where* (on the table). A preposition is often followed by a noun.

    Example: I live in *Japan.*
                  I drink tea *in the morning.*

Think of examples of each of these parts of speech.

Sentence Structure

Every English sentence must have at least two things: a *subject* (noun or pronoun) and a *verb.* Often an English sentence will have a subject, a verb and an *object* (also a noun or pronoun).

The most simple English sentence has this word order: subject−verb.

    Example: The *man runs.*

When a sentence has an object, the sentence has this word order: subject−verb−object.

    Example: I drink *tea.*

Sometimes, a sentence will have a preposition and noun after the verb.

    Example: I live *in Japan.*

Also, a preposition and noun can come after an object.

    Example: I drink tea *in the morning.*

Exercise C

Use the sentences or parts of the sentences that you wrote in Exercise B
to practice English sentence structure. The first one is done for you.

1. subject—verb

   __Einstein graduated.__
   _____

2. subject—verb—object

   _____

   _____

3. subject—verb—preposition + noun

   _____

   _____

4. subject—verb—object—preposition + noun

   _____

   _____

Exercise D

Sometimes, sentences will have two subjects, objects or verbs.

> *Examples:* *Albert* and *Mileva* married in 1903.
> Einstein enjoyed *philosophy* and *science.*
> Einstein *wrote* and *published* the "Theory of Relativity."
> Einstein *sailed boats* and *played* the *violin.*

There are two good sentences and two bad sentences below. One bad
sentence doesn't have a verb. The other bad sentence doesn't have a
subject or a verb. Circle the numbers of the good sentences. Change the
bad sentences and make good sentences.

1. Albert and Mileva in 1903.

2. Einstein died.

3. in 1933

4. Albert and Mileva had two sons.

Reading

The Life of Albert Einstein

Albert Einstein was a famous physicist and teacher. He worked to improve science and to help world peace. He cared about the people of the world.

Albert Einstein was born in Ulm, Germany on March 14, 1879. When he was young, Einstein didn't like school. He got poor grades in history, geography and languages. However, Einstein's two uncles helped him in science and math. Einstein's mother helped him to learn the violin. When he was older, Einstein studied physics in Zurich, Switzerland and graduated in 1900.

From 1902 to 1909, Einstein worked on his new, scientific ideas about space and time. He published an article on the "Theory of Relativity" in 1905. During this time, he also married his college sweetheart, Mileva Maric. They had two sons.

Einstein continued to work on his scientific ideas. In 1921, he won the Nobel Prize for physics. He also worked on his ideas for world peace. He traveled around the world and talked to people about peace. Einstein knew many famous philosophers and scientists. Everyone respected him.

Einstein left Germany in 1933. He thought Germany was going to start a war. He was right. World War II began in 1939. This was a difficult time for Einstein. He missed his friends and life in Europe. However, Einstein began a new life as a professor in an American university, Princeton. In 1940, he became an American citizen.

Einstein continued to teach and develop ideas in physics and to work for peace. He had a simple life. He played his violin and sailed his boat. He was shy and quiet, but he was considered one of the world's great men. Albert Einstein died on April 18, 1955. The people of the world will not forget this wonderful man.

Interpretation Check

Circle the letters of the sentences that are true.

1. Einstein's family:

   a. Einstein married three times.
   b. Einstein had three uncles.
   c. Einstein had two sons.

2. Einstein's education:

   a. Einstein loved school.
   b. Einstein was good in languages.
   c. Einstein graduated from college.

3. Einstein's work:

   a. Einstein was a professor, a scientist and a writer.
   b. Einstein taught history and geography.
   c. Einstein won the Nobel Prize for philosophy.

4. Einstein's interests:

   a. Einstein worked for world peace.
   b. Einstein liked noisy parties.
   c. Einstein played the piano and drove fast cars.

Question Structure

When you make questions in English, word order changes. If there is a verb for being, put the verb *before* the subject. Look at the first sentence of the reading:

Einstein was a famous physicist and teacher.

The question form for this sentence is:

Was Einstein a famous physicist and teacher?

If there is a verb for action, put DO or DID before the subject. The action verb stays in the same place and isn't changed for tense. Look at the third sentence of the reading:

He cared about the people of the world.

The question form for this sentence is:

Did he care about the people of the world?

These question forms are called *yes* and *no* questions.

...ask *who, what, when, where, why, how,* etc., put these
...he question. These questions are called **WH questions.**
...ntence:

Einstein left Germany in 1933.

A WH question for this sentence is:

When did Einstein leave Germany?

Exercise E

**Make *yes* and *no* questions from the sentences in the Interpretation
Check. The first one is done for you.**

1a. *Was Einstein married three times?*

1b. _____

1c. _____

2a. _____

2b. _____

2c. _____

3a. _____

3b. _____

3c. _____

4a. _____

4b. _____

4c. _____

Now change the *yes/no* questions to WH questions.

Exercise F

The paragraph below is a *summary* of "The Life of Albert Einstein."
A summary is a short version of a reading. A summary usually gives the important points of a reading. Fill in the blanks with the best word in the summary below.

Albert Einstein _____ a famous physicist and
                        (verb)

teacher. When he was young, he didn't like _____,
                                              (noun)

but when he was older, he studied physics. _____
                                              (pronoun)

worked on new ideas in physics. He won the Nobel Prize for physics

_____ 1921. Einstein also worked on ideas for world
(preposition)

peace. He left _____ in 1933 because this country
                 (noun)

was going to start a war. He _____ an American citizen
                               (verb)

in 1940. Einstein was a _____ man, but many people
                          (adjective)

think of him as one of the world's great men.

═══════════════════════ Let's Talk ═══════════════════════

In the charts below, you see events in the lives of famous people.
The charts are incomplete. In pairs, ask each other for the missing
information in each chart, and write the information in your chart.
Only look at *your* chart. Don't look at your partner's chart. Before
you begin, practice the question forms you will use. Answer in
complete sentences.

CHART A

Person	Born	Graduated	Married	Became	Retired	Died
Mao Tse-tung	1893		1920		1959	
Anwar el-Sadat		1938		president of Egypt 1970		1981
Shigeru Yoshida	1878		1938		1954	
Abraham Lincoln		didn't graduate		president of the U.S. 1861		1865

CHART B

Person	Born	Graduated	Married	Became	Retired	Died
Mao Tse-tung		1918		chairman of China 1949		1976
Anwar el-Sadat	1918		1949		didn't retire	
Shigeru Yoshida		1906		prime minister of Japan 1946		1967
Abraham Lincoln	1809		1842		didn't retire	

MY AUTOBIOGRAPHY

Exercise A

This is part of a college application for admission to an English as a Second Language program. Not all of the required information is on the application. What can you find out about the person who filled out this application? As a class, practice asking and answering questions about this person.

Office of International Education

Application for Admission
For students who speak English as a non-native language.

A. All students must complete this section of the application form.

1. Program (check one):
☒ Institute for the Study of American Language & Culture *only*
☐ Regular Undergraduate Program *only*
☐ ISALC *and* Regular Undergraduate Program

2. Plan to enter:
☒ Fall term   ☐ Winter term   ☐ Spring term   ☐ Summer term

3. Sex: ☒ Male ☐ Female   Marital status: ☒ Single ☐ Married   Will your spouse be with you? ☐ Yes ☐ No

4. Family name **Zaidan**   Given name **Nabeel**   Middle name

5. Complete address in your home country

6. Telephone number in your home country

7. Date of birth: Month   Day   Year **1965**   Country of birth **Kuwait**

8. Citizen of what country? **Jordan**

9. Will you need an I-20 to obtain a student (F-1) visa? ☒ Yes ☐ No

10. If you are currently in the U.S., what type of visa do you have?

11. Address of parents

12. Occupation of father **Builder**   Occupation of mother

13. Financial sponsor: ☐ Parents ☐ Self ☐ Other (If other, please give name and address of sponsor below.)
    Name

    Address

14. List in chronological order all schools you have *attended*—secondary or high schools and higher education.

Name of School	Location	Date of graduation

15. If you are not now attending school, state occupation **I was in the army**

16. Housing preference (please check one): ☒ On campus (dormitory) ☐ Off campus

Reading (student composition)

My Autobiography

My name is Nabeel. I was born in Kuwait in 1965. I lived in Kuwait for the first seven years of my life. My father worked for an oil company there. These years were very happy for my family.

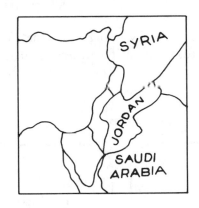

My family moved to Jordan in 1972 because my father retired from the oil company. Then, we started a new life in a poor country. My family wasn't rich in Jordan, but my father built apartments, and sometimes he made good money. During this time, I went to school. I enjoyed music and swimming. Also, I helped my father when I wasn't in school.

In 1981, I started to work in the summer. I had many different jobs. I worked in a pharmacy, for a medicine factory, and as a life guard. I worked as a life guard at swimming pools for five years. This was my favorite job. From 1984 to 1986, I was in the army. For three months, I learned to use a gun. After that, the army had me work as a lifeguard at a swimming pool for army men and their families.

On January 1, 1987, I moved to the U.S. to continue my education at an American university. Now, I am working very hard to learn English and to get a good score on the TOEFL test. The U.S. is a very nice, large country. I will stay here to get a university education and to visit every part of the U.S.

Nabeel Zaidan, Jordan

Interpretation Check

A good English writer doesn't write only sentences. A writer must learn to write paragraphs. A paragraph has more than one sentence. "My Autobiography" has four paragraphs. How many sentences are in the first paragraph? second? third? fourth? Each paragraph you write needs one important or general idea. In this exercise, circle the letter of the important idea in each paragraph.

1st paragraph: a. Nabeel's childhood in Kuwait
                     b. Nabeel's education

2nd paragraph: a. Nabeel's jobs
                     b. Nabeel's childhood in Jordan

3rd paragraph: a. Nabeel's future
                     b. Nabeel's jobs

4th paragraph: a. Nabeel's present life and future plans
                     b. Nabeel's family

Verb Tenses

In this chapter you get a very short introduction to the verb tenses that you will use in this text. Even if you are familiar with these tenses already, it is very important to know them well. The time line below gives you an idea of when and how to use verb tenses.

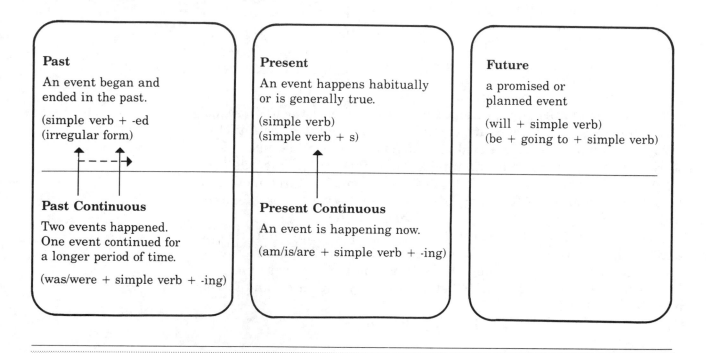

Past

An event began and ended in the past.

(simple verb + -ed)
(irregular form)

Past Continuous

Two events happened. One event continued for a longer period of time.

(was/were + simple verb + -ing)

Present

An event happens habitually or is generally true.

(simple verb)
(simple verb + s)

Present Continuous

An event is happening now.

(am/is/are + simple verb + -ing)

Future

a promised or planned event

(will + simple verb)
(be + going to + simple verb)

Exercise B

On the board, make a time line with dates in "My Autobiography." Write the events of Nabeel's life over the dates. For example, write "was born," "moved to Jordan," etc. Then, write at least five complete sentences about the time line. (Remember, a complete sentence must have a subject and a verb.)

1. _____

2. _____

3. _____

4. _____

5. _____

Exercise C

The paragraph below doesn't have punctuation. Punctuation means

periods: .
(Use periods at the end of sentences.)

capital letters: A B C D E F G H I J K L M N O P Q R S T U V W X Y Z
(Use capital letters at the beginning of sentences and for proper names.)

small letters: a b c d e f g h i j k l m n o p q r s t u v w x y z

question marks: ?
(Use questions marks at the end of sentences that are questions.)

commas: ,
(Use commas in the middle of two sentences when you want to connect
the sentences with *and, but, so, or.*)

**Read the paragraph. Where are the subjects and verbs? Put capital
letters in the beginning of the sentences and periods at the end of the
sentences.**

my father is a wonderful man he was born in Korea he grew up during two wars in Korea the first war was between Korea and Japan the
second war divided North Korea and South Korea many people were
poor and hungry my father didn't go to school because of these terrible
problems my father worked hard finally he went to school he graduated
from Gyong Buk University now he is a successful businessman and a
happy family man however he never forgets the troubles of his early life
the two wars made his personality very strong

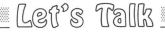

Make a time line of your life. Write important dates and events that
happened in your past. Write what you are doing now. Write a few
things you plan to do in the future. Don't write complete sentences.
(Your teacher might model a time line of his/her life for you on the board
before you begin.) You can use the space below, or if you need more
room, use another piece of paper.

Past	Present	Future

Events:

_____

Dates:

When you finish your time line, tell another student about your life.
Don't let the other student SEE your time line. The other student will
make *your* time line while you are talking. When you are finished talking, look at the time line of your life that the other student made.
Is it right? Then, the other student should tell you about his/her life.

Exercise D

On a piece of notebook paper, write 10 sentences about your partner's
life. Use the information you wrote on your partner's time line. Think
about what verb tense you need for each sentence.

Discussion Questions

Now it's time to get to know each other. You have five minutes to share
personal information with a partner. After five minutes, everyone must
switch partners even if you aren't finished. Before you start, it is a good
idea to review the question forms you will use.

1. Ask your partner's name and age.

2. Ask about your partner's interests.

3. Ask about your partner's education or jobs.

4. Ask about your partner's family.

Revision

Good writers write their compositions more than once. In this text, it is
recommended that you write each composition at least twice. Each time
you write a composition, it is called a *draft*. If you write a composition
three times, you will have a *first draft,* a *second draft,* and a *third draft*.
On these drafts you may receive "reader based" and "structure based"
comments. Reader based comments give you ideas on how to write a
more interesting and organized composition. Structure based comments
help you correct grammar and mechanics errors. Below is a suggested
correction symbol guide for structure based comments.

T	wrong verb tense	Pl	You need the plural noun
Agr	verb agreement problem	Sing	You need a singular noun
∧	You need a word	Inc	incomplete sentence
Sp	wrong spelling	____	You don't need a word (crossed out)
WW	wrong word	O	wrong punctuation (circled)

Sample Composition

Below is the first draft of the composition "My Autobiography." Grammar is not corrected, but there are reader based comments at the end.

I born in Kuwait in 1965. My family moved to Jordan in 1972 because my father retired from the oil company. This time I went to school I enjoy music and swimming. I worked as lifegard at swimming pools for five years in 1984 to 1986 I was in arme for two years. For three month I learned use gon. After that arme had me work as lifegard at a swimming pool for arme men and there family In January 1 1987 I move to U.S. to continue my education at an American university. Now, I working very hard to learn english and to get a good score on the TOEFL test.

Reader based comments:

This is very interesting. Please write more! Write in paragraph form:

1st paragraph: What is your name? What was life like in Kuwait for you and your family?

2nd paragraph: What was life like in Jordan for you and your family?

3rd paragraph: Did you have other jobs besides lifeguard? If so, what were they? Did you like them? When did you start to work?

4th paragraph: What do you think of the U.S.? What will you do in the future?

Here is the second draft. Grammar and mechanics errors are marked. Can you correct them? When you are finished, read "My Autobiography" and check your corrections.

My name is Nabeel. I born in Kuwait in 1965. I lived in Kuwait for the first seven years of my life. My father worked for an oil company there. This years very happy for my family.

My family moved to Jordan in 1972 because my father retired from the oil company. Then we start a new life in poor contry. My family wasn't rich in Jordan, but my father built apartment and sometimes he made good money. This time, I went to school I enjoy music and swimming. Also I helped my father when I wasn't in school.

In 1981, I start to work in summer. I had many different jobs. I worked in a farmasey, medesen factory, and a lifegard. I worked as lifegard at swimming pools for five years. This was my favorite job. In 1984 to 1986 I was in arme for two years. For three month I learned use gon. After that arme had me work as lifegard at a swimming pool for arme men and ther family.

In January 1 1987 I move to U.S. to continue my education at an American university. Now, I working very hard to learn english and get a good score on the TOEFL test. The U.S. is a very nice, large contry. I will stay here to get a university education and to visit every part of U.S.

C H A P T E R

2 Description I

Description is talking or writing about what people, places and things look like. In this chapter we will look at descriptions of national parks in the United States and other parts of the world. We will also look at a description of a young man named Stefano.

NATIONAL PARKS IN THE U.S.

Exercise A

Discuss the vocabulary below. Look at the map of the United States. Where are the national parks? What states are they in? What can you see in each national park?

mountains   geysers

volcano   caves

waterfalls   desert

canyon   forest

Exercise B

Use the vocabulary on the map to complete the sentences below.

Example: There are *mountains* in Grand Teton National Park.

1. There are _____ in Yosemite National Park.

2. There is a _____ in Redwood National Park.

3. There is a _____ in Big Bend National Park.

4. There is a _____ in Mt. Rainier National Park.

5. There are _____ in Shenendoah National Park.

6. There are _____ in Carlsbad Caverns National Park.

7. There are _____ in Yellowstone National Park.

8. There are _____ in The Great Smoky Mountains.

Reading

National Parks in the U.S.

The United States has many national parks. These parks are usually large and have beautiful scenery. There are mountains, rivers, waterfalls, forests, and canyons. Many national parks even have volcanoes. Two popular national parks in the United States are Yosemite National Park and the Great Smoky Mountains National Park.

Yosemite National Park is big. It covers 1,189 square miles. It is the size of the state of Rhode Island, but it isn't as big as Yellowstone National Park or as deep as the Grand Canyon! The park is located in mideastern California.

EL CAPITAN

There are many kinds of scenery in Yosemite. There is often snow on the rocky mountains. There are 770 miles of trails through these mountains. There are giant, old trees called sequoias. There are many high waterfalls and rocks. Some of these are so famous they have names. Bridalveil Fall is 620 feet high. El Capitan is 3,600 feet high. Many people do rock climbing on El Capitan. Another interesting sight is the animals. For example, there are many deer and bears. Campers tie their food in a tree, or the bears eat it. The bears even eat toothpaste!

The Great Smoky Mountains National Park is also a big park. It covers 812 square miles. The park is located on the eastern side of Tennessee and the western side of North Carolina. This park isn't as big as many other parks, but it has three times more visitors than other parks. Nine million people come here every year.

The Great Smoky Mountains have beautiful scenery. A lovely, green forest covers the high mountains. There are 900 miles of trails through this forest. Also, clouds and fog often cover the tops of the mountains. The clouds look like smoke. That is how this park got its name. There are more deer and bears here than in Yosemite. The black bears in The Great Smoky Mountains are very famous. They also love to try the food of campers and hikers. People need to be careful with their food, and not get too close to the bears.

There are national parks in half of the states in the United States. Each park has something beautiful and different to see. These parks are one of the United States' great treasures.

Interpretation Check

Circle the letter of the best answer.

1. An example of scenery is:
   a. a waterfall
   b. Tennessee
   c. Yosemite Park

2. An example of an animal is:
   a. a sequoia
   b. a bear
   c. a cloud

3. California is a:
   a. park
   b. trail
   c. state

4. Yosemite is a:
   a. park
   b. rock
   c. state

General & Specific

Words that are *general* refer to a group of things. Words that are *specific* refer to one kind of thing. Look for general and specific in your dictionary. What do they mean? Write the definition of each word below:

general: _____

specific: _____

PARK and ANIMAL are both general words. There are many kinds of parks and many kinds of animals. CALIFORNIA and YOSEMITE are both specific words. There is only one California and only one Yosemite.

Exercise C

Read "National Parks in the U.S." again. Then, look at the general words below. List the specific words that go with the general word. The first one is done for you.

1. Scenery	2. Animal	3. State
mountains	_____	_____
_____	_____	_____
_____	_____	_____
_____		

Think of other examples of general and specific words.

Present Tense

Present tense verbs are formed by adding *-s* or *-es* to the end of the simple verb after *he, she, it*. Present tense verbs after *I, you, we, they* stay in the simple form.

Use present tense when you want to talk about habitual or usual activities.

Examples: You drink coffee every morning. He drinks coffee every morning.
Do you drink coffee every morning? Does he drink coffee every morning?
When do you drink coffee? When does he drink coffee?

Use *don't* and *doesn't* with the simple verb when you want to use *not* in present tense:

They don't study in the library. She doesn't study in the library.
Do they study in the library? Does she study in the library?

Present tense *be* verbs: *am, is, are*

Examples: I am usually happy. He is in the house.
Are you usually happy? Is he in the house?
Why are you usually happy? Where is he?

Note: The verb *have* changes to *has* after *he, she* and *it.*

Spelling

Add *-es* when a verb ends in *-sh, -ch, -ss, -x.* Also, when a verb ends in *-y* after a consonant, change the *y* to *i* and add *es.* For example, *study–studies.* When a verb ends in *-y* after a vowel, only add *s.* For example, *play–plays.*

Exercise D

Complete the sentences below with the correct form of the present tense verb. The first sentence is done for you.

1. The United States _____*has*_____ many national parks. (have)

2. Yosemite and The Great Smoky Mountains _____ two popular national parks. (be)

3. Yosemite _____ in mideastern California. (be)

4. There _____ many high waterfalls and rocks in Yosemite. (be)

5. There _____ many deer and bears. (be)

6. The Great Smoky Mountains Park _____ as big as other parks. (be, not)

7. A lovely forest _____ the high mountains. (cover)

8. The bears in the Great Smoky Mountains _____ the food of campers. (love)

9. Each park _____ something beautiful and different. (have)

There Is and There Are

In English, when you describe a place, you often use *there is* or *there are*. The subject of the sentence is the noun that follows the *be* verb. For example, you can say: Snow is on the rocky mountains. Snow is the singular subject of the sentence. Or you can say: There is snow on the rocky mountains. Snow is still the subject. You can say: National parks are in half of the states. National parks is the plural subject of the sentence. Or you can say: There are national parks in half of the states. When you make a question using *there is* or *there are*, put the *be* verb before *there:* Is there snow on the rocky mountains? Are there national parks in half of the states?

Exercise E

Change the sentences in Exercise D to *yes* and *no* questions. If a sentence has a *be* verb, use *is* or *are* in the question. If a sentence has a *do* verb, use *do* or *does* in the question.

1. _____

2. _____

3. _____

4. _____

5. _____

6. _____

7. _____

8. _____

9. _____

Paragraph Form

When you write in English, you must use paragraph form. A paragraph must have at least two or three sentences. A good paragraph can have three sentences or twenty, but each paragraph should have one general idea. This idea is called the topic or the main idea of a paragraph. Also, you must *indent* each paragraph. To indent, move the first word of your first sentence over five letter spaces. You must move the first word of <u>every</u> new paragraph. Look at "National Parks in the U.S." How many paragraphs do you see? What is the first word of every paragraph?

Exercise F: Summary

Copy the sentences in Exercise D in paragraph form. Make <u>one</u> paragraph. You don't need to add your own sentences. Don't write numbers. Indent the first word of your first sentence.

Pair Work: You should look only at Chart A, while your partner looks only at Chart B. Ask each other for the missing information in each chart, and write the information in your chart. Before you start, review with your teacher how to ask and answer questions using the grammar points discussed in this chapter. Also, review the pronunciation of the names of the places you will talk about. If you can't pronounce words in the chart, ask your teacher, or spell the words for your partner. When you are finished, review the charts as a class. This task is especially interesting if you can use a large world map or atlas.

CHART A
National Parks in the World

Place	Location	Size	Scenery
Serengeti National Park		100 miles wide 130 miles long	
Hawaii Volcanoes National Park	southern Hawaii		volcanoes
Ujung Kulon National Park	Indonesia Java Island		rare animals volcano
Tikal National Park		144 square miles	
Kanha National Park	central India		rare tigers

CHART B
National Parks in the World

Place	Location	Size	Scenery
Serengeti National Park	mideastern Africa Tanzania		over two million large animals
Hawaii Volcanoes National Park		358 square miles	
Ujung Kulon National Park		294 square miles	
Tikal National Park	northern Guatemala		1,700 year old Mayan city
Kanha National Park		362 square miles	

Exercise G

On a piece of notebook paper, write one paragraph about two places.
Choose two places from the chart. Begin your paragraph with a general
sentence, for example: Serengeti National Park and Tikal National Park
are very interesting places. Write about the place, location, size and
scenery of each park. You will only need the information in your chart.

STEFANO

Exercise A

Before you start, you or your teacher can bring in pictures of people in photographs, books, or magazines. Describe the people in the pictures using the vocabulary below:

Build	Height	Hair	Age	Face
heavy	tall	fair	old	happy
strong	medium	dark	middle-aged	sad
medium	short	curly	teen-aged	kind
small		wavy	young	mean
thin		straight		serious
		short		
		long		

Exercise B

Look at the picture below. It is a picture of a man named Stefano. Read the paragraph describing Stefano. Fill in the blanks with vocabulary from the list above.

Stefano is attractive. He is _____ (build) because he

did judo for a long time. He isn't _____ (height), but he

isn't short either. His hair is _____ and

_____ . His face is usually _____

because he loves to live.

Reading (student composition)

Stefano

I have known Stefano for a long time. We are good friends. We are almost like brothers. I remember when we went to elementary school and already we were bound. Now, our friendship isn't changed with time. It is stronger.

Stefano is attractive. He is strong because he did judo for a long time. He isn't tall, but he isn't short either. His hair is straight and dark. His eyes are brown, and his complexion is dark. His face is usually happy because he loves to live, to joke, to learn new things, to travel, and to dream.

People like Stefano because his personality is kind and strong. If you need a favor, he doesn't back out. He doesn't judge people before he knows their story. He likes to make decisions quickly. Sometimes, our friends call him the "boss." However, sometimes people around him change his ideas.

Stefano and I do many things together. We play each kind of sport because both of us have an athletic build. Unfortunately, we smoke cigarettes, so we are a little limited! Also, we have the same love for fast cars. Sometimes we compete to see who is the best driver. Finally, we listen to the same music.

Stefano and I are different. For example, I like to study because every time I begin a book, a new world opens in front of my eyes. Stefano hates to study or to read a simple book. He likes motorcycles more than I do, and I like soccer more than he does. However, differences don't change our friendship.

This is only a short description of Stefano. I want to write many other things, but I need to write for hours to do a good description. I think it is enough to understand the friendship which binds us.

Armando Ezio Ferrari, Italy

Main Ideas and Details

When you read, try to find the *main ideas* of the reading. Usually, every paragraph has one main idea. The main idea is the most important or general idea of the paragraph. You can often find the main idea of a paragraph in the first sentence of the paragraph. The other sentences in a paragraph contain *details*. Details are more specific than main ideas. They help explain a main idea or give examples of a main idea.

Note: The main idea is sometimes also called the *topic*. In this text, we will use *main idea*.

Interpretation Check

Read "Stefano" again. There are six paragraphs. Each paragraph has a main idea. Read the choices below. Circle the letter of the main idea for each paragraph.

1. Main idea of 1st paragraph:
   a. Stefano and Armando are good friends.
   b. They went to elementary school.
   c. The friendship isn't changed.

2. Main idea of 2nd paragraph:
   a. He isn't short.
   b. His face is happy.
   c. Stefano is attractive.

3. Main idea of 3rd paragraph:
   a. He doesn't judge people.
   b. Stefano's personality is kind and strong.
   c. Friends call him "boss."

4. Main idea of 4th paragraph:
   a. Stefano and Armando do many things together.
   b. They play sports.
   c. They love cars.

5. Main idea of 5th paragraph:
   a. Stefano hates to study.
   b. Stefano and Armando are different.
   c. Armando likes soccer.

6. Main idea of 6th paragraph:
   a. Armando wants to write more.
   b. This is a short description.
   c. Armando needs more hours to write.

Exercise C

More practice with main ideas: Read "National Parks in the U.S." again. In the exercise below, there are two sentences from each paragraph. One sentence gives the main idea, and one sentence gives a detail. Write main idea or detail next to each sentence. The first one is done for you.

1. 1st paragraph:

   a) The United States has many national parks.

   main idea

   b) Two popular parks in the United States are Yosemite National Park and the Great Smoky Mountains National Park.

   _____

2. 2nd paragraph:

   a) It covers 1,189 square miles. _____

   b) Yosemite National Park is big. _____

3. 3rd paragraph:

   a) There are many high waterfalls and rocks.

   _____

   b) There are many kinds of scenery in Yosemite.

   _____

4. 4th paragraph:

   a) Nine million people come here every year.

   _____

   b) The Great Smoky Mountains National Park is also a big park.

   _____

5. 5th paragraph:

   a) The Great Smoky Mountains have beautiful scenery.

   _____

   b) A lovely, green forest covers the high mountains.

   _____

Predicate Adjectives

When you describe a person or a place, you use adjectives. Often, an adjective comes before the noun it describes, for example: Susan has dark hair. *Dark* is an adjective. It describes *hair* which is a noun. Sometimes, adjectives are used after a *be* verb (*is, am, are*). These adjectives are called *predicate adjectives*, for example: Susan's hair is dark. Often, you can use adjectives in these two ways. If you use *have* or *has* in a sentence, you can put an adjective before the noun: John has a serious face. If you use *is, am* or *are* in a sentence, put the adjective after the be verb: John's face is serious.

Note: You don't need to use adjectives with the nouns *height, weight,* or *age*. For example, you can say:

She is short. He is thin. I am young.

Exercise D

Rewrite the sentences below using predicate adjectives.

1. Stefano has a strong build.

   _____

2. He has straight hair.

   _____

3. He has a happy face.

   _____

4. The United States has large national parks.

   _____

5. The Great Smoky Mountains have beautiful scenery.

   _____

Exercise E

Now, change the sentences below using *have* or *has*.

1. Jane's hair is blond and straight.

   _____

2. Mike's build is heavy.

   _____

3. Ann's eyes are brown.

_____

4. Jack's beard is very thick and curly.

_____

5. Ed's moustache is long and thin.

_____

6. Debbie's clothes are expensive.

_____

7. Bill's sweater is blue.

_____

Let's Talk

Pair Work: You should look only at Picture A while the other student looks only at Picture B. Describe the people in the picture to each other: build, height, hair, age, and face. Circle the differences in build, height, hair and face in each person. (The ages are the same in both pictures.) For example, in Picture A, David has a beard. In picture B, David doesn't have a beard. On both pictures, circle the place on his face where his beard is or isn't. Then, compare pictures and discuss the differences in class.

Nancy   David   Ann   Pat   Mike   Jane

Exercise F

On another piece of paper, write a paragraph. Describe your partner.
Write about your partner's build, height, hair, age and face. Begin your
paragraph with a sentence that gives your partner's name, for example:
My partner's name is _____ .

Discussion Questions

Talk about these questions in small groups or with a partner. Talking
about these questions will give you more conversation practice. Also,
you might get some good ideas for your next composition.

1. Can you describe national parks or other scenic areas in your
   country?

2. Have you been to scenic areas in the United States or in other parts
   of the world? Describe them.

3. How would you describe your favorite actor, singer, or sports player?
   How would you describe your brother or sister? How would you
   describe yourself?

Composition: Description

For your first composition, you can describe places or people. If you
have a lot to say about one place or one person, just write about one.
You should write at least two paragraphs, but if you have more to say,
write three or four. Remember, each paragraph needs one main idea.

Exercise G: Pre-Writing

Look at the two sample topics below. Discuss the main ideas with your
teacher. What details could go with these main ideas? Then, think of
your own topic. What are your main ideas?

Topic 1: My Family

1st paragraph main idea: *people in my family* _____

details: *how many people are there? names?* _____

2nd paragraph main idea: *parents* _____

details: _____

3rd paragraph main idea: *brothers and sisters* _____

details: _____

Topic 2: A Beautiful Place in My Country

1st paragraph main idea: *where is it?* _____

details: _____

2nd paragraph main idea: *what is the scenery?* _____

details: _____

What is your topic? What are your main ideas? Write the first draft of
your composition.

Before you turn in your composition, check it, or have a partner check it. Use the questions below to help you. Talk to your teacher about your composition after you have turned it in. Discuss what you wrote below.

1. Does each paragraph have a main idea? YES NO

    Write the main idea of each paragraph:

    _____

    _____

    _____

2. Do you use present tense correctly? YES NO

3. Do you use predicate adjectives correctly? YES NO

4. Do you use paragraph form? YES NO

5. Try to think of two more details you could add to this topic and write them below:

    _____

    _____

6. What do you think are the most interesting ideas or details in this composition?

    _____

    _____

3 Description II

In Chapter 2 we used present tense verbs to describe places and people. In this chapter, we will use a new verb tense, present continuous. First, we will describe the life of an American family. Then, we will describe a restaurant called American Espresso.

AN AMERICAN FAMILY

Exercise A

Look at the picture above. Then, match the phrases on the left with the phrases on the right. Write complete sentences on the lines below.

1. Their son, Christopher, is eating cereal   in their kitchen

2. Their daughter, Kimberly, is talking and leaning at the table

3. His wife, Carol, is sitting and studying   behind the counter

4. Don Lohrey is washing breakfast dishes   across the table from her

5. An American family is preparing for the day against the wall

1. _____

2. _____

3. _____

4. _____

5. _____

Present Continuous Tense

Present continuous verbs are formed by adding *-ing* to the end of the simple verb. You also need to put a present tense *be* verb before the simple verb. You don't need to use present continuous tense very often. Use it when you want to talk about activities that are happening *now*.

Examples: You are reading now.   He isn't sitting in a classroom.
          You're reading now.   Is he sitting in a classroom?
          Are you reading now?
          What are you reading now?

Note: Verbs that describe feelings and senses such as *like, love, hate, see, hear, taste, smell* are rarely used in present continuous form.

Spelling:

1. A verb with one syllable, one consonant at the end of the syllable, and one vowel next to the consonant doubles the final letter. For example, the final letter of these verbs are all doubled: sit, hop, plan, rob.

2. When a verb ends in *e*, drop the *e* and add *ing*. For example, the final *e* of these verbs are all dropped: make, write, live, lose.

Exercise B

Write a paragraph. Put the sentences you wrote in Exercise A in correct order. Which sentence should come first? second? third? fourth? fifth? Don't write numbers. Remember to indent your first word.

_____

_____

_____

_____

_____

_____

Reading

An American Family

The Lohrey family is a typical middle-class American family. Don is 41 years old. He is a manager of a computer store. Carol is also 41 years old. She works in the office of a large sports equipment company. She and Don have two children: 13-year old Kimberly and 9-year old Christopher.

Everyday, this family is very busy with school and work activities, but they always try to spend time together. They usually go to church on Sunday, and they are often busy with church activities such as special dinners or choir practice. Sometimes, Carol teaches a class for her church. This family loves sports. Kimberly and Christopher always play baseball in the spring and summer, soccer in the fall, and basketball in the winter. Carol and Don often run three or four miles together. They run to stay in shape and to take a break from their busy schedule.

Here is a picture of the Lohrey family preparing for the day. The family is in the kitchen. Don is washing the breakfast dishes behind the counter. Carol is sitting and studying for her class at the table. Christopher is eating cereal across from her. Christopher is growing so fast he has to eat a lot. Kimberly is leaning against the wall and talking on the telephone to one of her many girlfriends. She is holding the dog, Abigail. They are all doing different things, but they are together, so the morning is a good time for them.

American family life is slowly changing. Fifty years ago, people usually had more than two children. Only the husband had a job outside the home. The wife took care of the home and raised the children. Now, more American women are getting more education for better jobs. Many American men are spending more time at home. They share the jobs of housework and child-raising with their wives. These changes are sometimes difficult for people to accept. It is important to people, like the Lohreys, to keep some traditional values in a busy, changing world.

Interpretation Check

There are four paragraphs in "An American Family." What is the main idea of each paragraph? Circle the letter of the best answer.

1. Main idea of the 1st paragraph:
   a. Don is a manager.
   b. introduction of the Lohrey family
   c. They have two children.

2. Main idea of the 2nd paragraph:
   a. They usually go to church.
   b. Carol and Don often run.
   c. the family's daily activities

3. Main idea of the 3rd paragraph:
   a. what the family is doing in the picture
   b. Christopher is eating cereal.
   c. Kimberly is leaning against the wall.

4. Main idea of the 4th paragraph:
   a. American women are getting more education.
   b. American men are spending time at home.
   c. American family life is changing.

Exercise C

Read the sentences below from "An American Family." If the sentence is true, circle T. If the sentence is false, circle F and change the sentence so that it is true.

1. The Lohreys rarely go to church on Sunday.   T   F

   _____

2. They are never busy with church activities.   T   F

   _____

3. Carol and Don often run three or four miles together.   T   F

   _____

4. Fifty years ago, people seldom had more than two children.   T   F

   _____

5. These changes are sometimes difficult for people to accept.   T   F

   _____

Frequency Adverbs

When you want to tell *how often* something happens, use frequency adverbs: *always, usually, often, sometimes, rarely/seldom, never.* These adverbs come <u>before</u> a present or past tense verb and <u>after</u> a present or past tense *be* verb.

> *Examples:*   He *usually* studies at the library.
> He is *usually* at the library on Wednesday night.

always = 100%, usually/often = 90%–75%, sometimes = 50%, rarely/seldom = 10%, never = 0%

Note: Frequency adverbs are not generally used with present continuous tense.

Exercise D: Summary

Read the summary below of "An American Family." Fill in the blanks with the present tense or the present continuous verb form.

The Lohrey family _____ (be) a typical American

family. Everyday, this family _____ (be) very busy with

school and work activities, but they always _____ (try)

to spend time together. Now, American family life _____

(change). More women _____ (work) outside the home,

and more men _____ (share) housework. These

changes _____ (be) sometimes difficult to accept.

The Lohreys _____ (accept) the changes, but also they

_____ (keep) some traditional values.

Exercise E

Use the answers on the right to make questions about the summary. If the answer begins with a yes or no, make a *yes/no* question. If the answer doesn't begin with a yes or no, make a WH question.

1. _____ Yes, the Lohrey family is a
   typical American family.

2. _____ Yes, American family life
   is changing.

3. _____ Women work outside the
   home.

4. _____ Men share housework.

5. _____ The Lohreys keep
   traditional values.

In "An American Family" you read a little about the daily life of the Lohreys. In the charts below, you see the daily schedule of Susan, a university student. The charts are incomplete. In pairs, ask each other for the missing information in each chart, and write the information in your chart.

You need to ask two questions: It is (time/day). What is Susan doing now?

How often does Susan (present tense verb)?

You answer the first question with a present continuous verb.
You answer the second question with a frequency adverb and a present tense verb.
For example, look at Susan's schedule for Monday.

Question: It is 8:30 on Monday. What is Susan doing now?

Answer: She is driving to school.

Question: How often does Susan drive to school?

Answer: She usually drives to school. (4 days a week)

CHART A
Susan's Daily Schedule

	Monday	Tuesday	Wednesday	Thursday	Friday
8:30	drives to school	drives to school	drives to school	drives to school	
9:00	takes math class		takes math class		
11:00					
1:00		studies in library		studies in library	
3:00	works in a store	works in a store	works in a store	works in a store	works in a store
6:00					goes to a restaurant
9:00	studies	studies	studies	studies	
11:00	watches the news	watches the news	watches the news		

CHART B
Susan's Daily Schedule

	Monday	Tuesday	Wednesday	Thursday	Friday
8:30					sleeps late
9:00		takes biology class		takes biology class	walks to school
11:00	takes economics class	takes economics class	takes economics class	takes economics class	takes economics class
1:00	takes dance class		takes dance class		takes dance class
3:00					
6:00	makes dinner	makes dinner	makes dinner	makes dinner	
9:00					meets with friends
11:00				stays up late	dances at a disco

Exercise F

On a piece of notebook paper, write about *your* daily schedule from Monday to Friday. Your first sentence should say something general about your schedule. For example, are your days busy? relaxed? boring? interesting? What are you doing now: taking classes at a university? taking a break from school or a job in your country to study English? studying for the TOEFL? Then, describe your days: what do you do everyday? Use frequency adverbs and present tense. Suggestion: If your schedule is very busy, you will probably need to write at least two paragraphs. Don't forget to indent the first word of each paragraph.

Exercise A

With your teacher, describe the picture above. What is it a picture of? How many people and things do you see? Where are they? What are the people doing? You will need to use *there is/are* and prepositions: in, on, at, behind, next to, across from, inside, outside, on the right, on the left, in the middle, in the corner, etc. You will also need to use present continuous tense.

Exercise B

Tell your teacher to close his/her book. Now, describe the picture to your teacher. Your teacher will draw the picture on the board. Don't let your teacher look at the picture! Your description must be very clear or your teacher will make mistakes. Students should take turns describing where people and things are and what people are doing. Have fun with this exercise.

Reading (student composition)

American Espresso

I am sitting in a restaurant called American Espresso. It is on the corner of Sixth Avenue and Hall Street. Because American Espresso is such a nice place, many people come here to eat, talk and study.

At this moment, I am looking around me, and I see a lot of things. There are several tables in this restaurant. There are three round tables on the right, next to the window, and two round tables on the left. There are two rectangular tables in the middle of the restaurant. There is a glass counter in the middle of the restaurant. There is a lot of food inside the counter. There are a lot of doughnuts and croissants and a few muffins. A menu is hanging on the wall, behind the counter, and three pictures are hanging on the wall, next to the menu. There is a door in the corner, on the right.

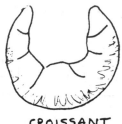

CROISSANT

There are a lot of people here right now because it is breakfast time. Many people are sitting at the tables. Some people are talking and drinking coffee. A few people, all students, are writing a composition for their writing class. Two waiters are working. One waiter is behind the counter. He is helping two people who want food or coffee. The other waiter is cleaning the table near the door.

It is a beautiful day, so there are many people outside the restaurant. The sun is shining, and the temperature is warm. A few people are walking on the sidewalk outside the restaurant. Several people are waiting at a bus stop to go downtown. There aren't any cars on the street. Maybe everyone likes to walk or take a bus on a pretty day.

Inside and outside the restaurant, all the people are busy. They are working, talking, dreaming and enjoying the day.

Carlos Pitty, Panama

Topic Sentences

Every paragraph needs a main idea. A good writer will tell the reader what the main idea of a paragraph is in a *topic sentence*. A topic sentence is often the first sentence in a paragraph. When you write, practice putting a topic sentence first. Since a topic sentence gives the reader the main idea of a paragraph, the topic sentence should be *general*.

Note: The topic sentence is sometimes also called the main idea sentence. In this text we will use *topic sentence*.

Interpretation Check

Read "American Espresso" again. The first sentence of each paragraph is a topic sentence. Look at the topic sentences below. Then, circle the main ideas that go with the topic sentences.

1. 1st paragraph topic sentence:
   I am sitting in a restaurant called "American Espresso."

   1st paragraph main idea:
   a. where the writer is
   b. things in the restaurant
   c. what people eat

2. 2nd paragraph topic sentence:
   At this moment, I am looking around me, and I see a lot of things.

   2nd paragraph main idea:
   a. tables in the restaurant
   b. food in the restaurant
   c. things in the restaurant

3. 3rd paragraph topic sentence:
   There are a lot of people here right now because it is breakfast time.

   3rd paragraph main idea:
   a. waiters in the restaurant
   b. people in the restaurant
   c. students in the restaurant

4. 4th paragraph topic sentence:
   There are also many people outside the restaurant because it is a beautiful day.

   4th paragraph main idea:
   a. people on the sidewalk
   b. people outside the restaurant
   c. people at the bus stop

5. 5th paragraph topic sentence:
   Inside and outside the restaurant, all the people are busy.

   5th paragraph main idea:
   a. people are working
   b. people are talking
   c. people inside and outside the restaurant

Exercise C

Look at the picture of "American Espresso." Then, use two prepositional phrases to describe the location of the people or things below. Remember to put a comma between the prepositional phrases. If you use *there is* or *there are* with present continuous, change the word order. The subject comes between the *be* verb and the *-ing* verb. The first sentence is done for you.

1. plant: *A plant is hanging from the ceiling, on the left.*

   (or): *There is a plant hanging from the ceiling, on the left.*

2. waiter: _____

3. menu: _____

4. students: _____

5. pictures: _____

Count and Non Count Nouns

In English, plural nouns end in *-s* or *-es*, for example: pencils, boxes, dictionaries. These nouns are called *count* nouns. Some nouns don't have a plural form because they usually aren't counted, for example: water, air, homework. These nouns are called *non count* nouns.

> Count nouns go with these quantifiers: *many, a few*
> Non count nouns go with these quantifiers: *much, a little*
> Both count and non count nouns go with *a lot of, some, any*

many, much, several, a lot of = a large amount or number
some = indefinite amount or number (less than many or much, more than a few or a little)
a few, a little = a small amount or number
any = none (*Any* is used in negative statements and in questions.)

Note: Use a singular *be* verb with a non count noun, for example: "There *is* a little coffee."

The noun *people* looks like a non count noun, but it is treated like a plural count noun.

Exercise D

Look at the picture below again. Then use quantifiers to complete the sentences.

1. There are _____ tables in this restaurant.

2. There is _____ food inside the counter.

3. There are _____ doughnuts and croissants.

4. There are _____ muffins.

5. There are _____ people here right now.

6. _____ people are sitting at the tables.

7. _____ people are talking and drinking coffee.

8. _____ people, all students, are writing a composition.

9. _____ people are waiting at a bus stop to go downtown.

10. There aren't _____ cars on the street.

Articles

A, an and the are articles. Use a before singular count nouns that begin with a consonant, for example: a restaurant. Use an before singular count nouns that begin with a vowel, for example: an apple. Use a and an when you are writing about a noun for the first time or when a noun is nonspecific.

> *Example:* I eat in a restaurant every day. (We don't know <u>which</u> restaurant. It isn't a specific restaurant.)

Use *the* before specific count and non count nouns.

> *Example:* I eat in *the* restaurant on Main Street and 2nd Avenue. (We know which restaurant because there can only be <u>one</u> restaurant at this address.)

Don't use articles before *nonspecific* plural count nouns and non count nouns.

> *Examples:* I eat in restaurants several times a week.
> I eat fish several times a week.

How could you change the sentences above so that you would need to use articles?

Exercise E

Fill in the blanks below with *a, an, the,* or nothing. Don't worry if you feel two answers are right. Sometimes, you can use both *a* and *the* if you have good reasons.

I see a lot of things in the American Espresso Restaurant. There are several tables in this restaurant. There is _____ glass counter in the middle. There is a lot of food inside _____ counter. _____ menu is hanging on _____ wall behind _____ counter, and three pictures are hanging on _____ wall next to _____ menu. There is _____ door in the corner, on the right.

There are a lot of people here. Many people are sitting at _____ tables. Some people are drinking _____ coffee. Two waiters are working. One waiter is behind _____ counter. _____ other waiter is cleaning _____ table near _____ door.

Sentence Combining

When you write English, you will often combine two or three sentences to make one sentence. Sentences are often combined with **connecting words** such as *because, and, but, so, if, when, before, after.* There are a few rules to remember when you use these words:

1. Do not begin a sentence with *and, but, so.* These connecting words combine two or three sentences in the middle. A comma goes before the connecting word. (In your reading, you may find that this rule is somewhat flexible.)

    Examples: a) San Francisco is in a beautiful location, *and* the weather there is very nice.
    b) Los Angeles has many interesting sights, *but* the pollution is terrible.
    c) The pollution in Los Angeles is terrible, *so* we go to San Francisco for vacations.
    d) Los Angeles has many interesting sights, *but* the pollution is terrible, *so* we go to San Francisco for vacations.

What single sentences have been combined in the examples above?
What are the subjects and verbs in each example?

Note: If the first single sentence in a combination has four words or fewer, the comma is often dropped.

2. *Because, if, when, before,* and *after* can go in the beginning of a sentence combination or in the middle. If they go in the beginning, always put a comma after the first clause. If they go in the middle, don't use a comma.

    Examples: a) John practices tennis everyday *because* he wants to be a tennis coach.
    Because John wants to be a tennis coach, he practices tennis everyday.
    b) Your English is good *if* you understand this example.
    If you understand this example, your English is good.
    c) Ann always writes a topic sentence *when* she writes a paragraph.
    When Ann writes a paragraph, she always writes a topic sentence.
    d) Ann always writes a topic sentence *when* she writes a paragraph *because* she wants to be a good writer, *but* she thinks topic sentences are difficult.

What single sentences have been combined in the examples above?
What are the subjects and verbs in each example?

Exercise F

Combine the sentences below with the connecting word in parentheses.
Be careful. Make sure that your combination makes sense.

1. American Espresso is such a nice place. Many people come here to eat.   (because)

   _____

2. I am looking around me. I see a lot of things.   (and)

   _____

3. A menu is hanging on the wall. Three pictures are hanging on the wall.   (and)

   _____

4. There are a lot of people here. It is breakfast time.   (because)

   _____

5. There are also many people outside the restaurant. It is a beautiful day.   (so)

   _____

=================== Let's Talk ===================

Pair Work: You should look only at Picture A while your partner looks only at Picture B. Describe the rooms in the pictures to each other. How many people and things do you see? Where are they? What are the people doing? There are nine differences between Picture A and Picture B. When you find a difference, circle it on your picture.

Exercise G

On another piece of paper, write two paragraphs. Describe your classroom. In the first paragraph, describe where things are. In the second paragraph, describe where people are and what they are doing. Don't forget to begin each paragraph with a topic sentence.

Discussion Questions

Talk about these questions in small groups or with a partner. Talking about these questions will give you more conversation practice. Also, you might get some good ideas for your next composition.

1. What is the daily schedule in your family? For example, what do your mother and father usually do every day? If you have brothers and sisters, what do they usually do? What are they doing now?

2. Is your family a typical family in your country? Why or why not?

3. Describe your family's house, or the house or apartment you live in now. How many rooms are there? Describe where a few things are in each room.

Composition: Description

For this composition, describe a place. You can make a short "field trip"
as a class to a location such as a restaurant or park, or you can choose
your own location, such as a hotel lobby or museum.

Exercise H: Pre-Writing

Before you write, look at the main idea questions below. Write down
some details. Try to put down a lot of details. Then, write a composition.
Each paragraph should have a topic sentence.

1. Where are you? What do people usually do here?

   details: _____

   _____

   _____

2. What things do you see? Where are they?

   details: _____

   _____

   _____

3. What are people doing?

   details: _____

   _____

   _____

4. How do you feel about this place? Is it typical? interesting? useful?
   beautiful? Why?

   details: _____

   _____

   _____

Before you turn in your composition, check it, or have a partner check it. Use the questions below to help you. Talk to your teacher about your composition after you have turned it in. Discuss what you wrote below.

1. Does each paragraph have a main idea?   YES   NO

   Write the main idea of each paragraph:

   _____

   _____

   _____

   _____

2. Do you use present continuous correctly?   YES   NO

3. Do you use prepositional phrases correctly?   YES   NO

4. Do you combine sentences correctly?   YES   NO

5. Try to think of three more details you could add to this topic and write them below:

   _____

   _____

   _____

6. What do you think are the most interesting ideas or details in this composition?

   _____

   _____

4 Process Description

In this chapter, we will do a different kind of description called process description. Process description tells how to do something or how something works. First, we will describe how to make a pencil holder. Then, we will describe how to use the telephone in the U.S.

HOW TO MAKE A PENCIL HOLDER

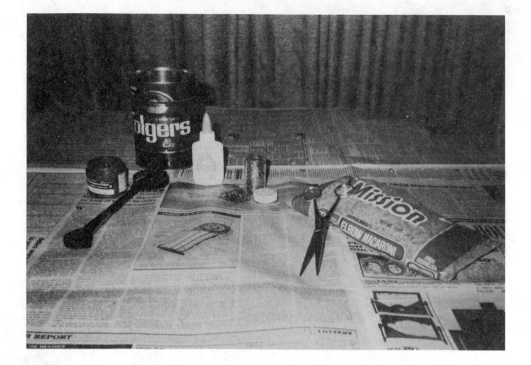

Exercise A

Look at the picture. What do you need to make a pencil holder? How much of each thing, or how many things do you need? Fill in the blanks with these words: *a, some, a few, a little, a lot of, much, many*.

1. You need _____ can.

2. You need _____ macaroni.

3. You need _____ glue.

4. You need _____ paint.

5. You need _____ paintbrush.

6. You need _____ glitter.

Imperatives

When you describe a process, tell someone how to do something, you can use imperatives. Imperatives give commands. The subject of an imperative sentence is always *you*, but *you* isn't used in the sentence. For example, when you tell someone to sit down, you can say: You sit down or Sit down. The second sentence is an imperative. Teachers often use imperatives when talking to students, for example: "Open your books." "Take out a piece of paper.", and "Write on the board." With your teacher, think of some other imperatives you use in the classroom.

Note: If you use words like *can, should, must, will* in a sentence, *you* must be used as the subject: Turn off the radio or You should turn off the radio.

Exercise B

Change the sentences below into imperatives. The first one is done for you.

1. First, she gets a can and a bottle of glue.

   First, get a can and a bottle of glue.

2. She paints the macaroni with a paintbrush.

   _____

3. She pours a lot of glue all over the can.

   _____

4. Finally, she sprinkles some glitter on the paint.

   _____

5. Then, she puts a lot of macaroni on the can.

   _____

Sequence Words

When you tell someone how to do something, you can use *sequence words: first, then, next, after that, finally.* These words come at the beginning of a sentence. You use these words to show order. For example, you can use sequence words to show time order. Look at the list of things to do in the morning. What do you do first? next? finally?

Things To Do In The Morning

get dressed   drink coffee

take a bath   brush my teeth

eat breakfast   cook breakfast

Note: You don't need to use a sequence word in every sentence.

Exercise C

The sentences in Exercise B are not in good order. Put them in good order. Write a paragraph.

Begin with this topic sentence: "It is fun to make a pencil holder."

_____

_____

_____

_____

_____

_____

_____

_____

_____

Reading

How to Make a Pencil Holder

You will read an interview in which Sydney Kinnaman describes how to make a pencil holder. As you read, think about these questions: What things do you need to make a pencil holder? What do you do to make a pencil holder? What do you do with a pencil holder after you have made it?

Sydney: Today, I will show you how to make a pencil holder. Everyone needs a pencil holder. If you are a student, a doctor, a businessman, or a truck driver, you need a pencil holder to hold your pencils.

Interviewer: What things do you need to make a pencil holder?

Sydney: What you need first of all is a can, a simple coffee can. You need a bag of macaroni. You need a bottle of glue. Also, you need a jar of glitter and a jar of paint. Don't forget a pair of scissors and one paintbrush.

Interviewer: How do you make a pencil holder?

Sydney: First, get glue, and pour glue all over the can.

Interviewer: All over the can?

Sydney: Yes, pour glue all over the can, but never under the can. If you pour glue under the can, you will stick the can to the table you are working on. Don't use a lot of glue. Just use a little.

Interviewer: What do you do next?

Sydney: After you pour the glue around the can, open the bag of macaroni with the scissors. Then, put several pieces of macaroni on the can. You can use any design.

Interviewer: What do you do then?

Sydney: Then, sprinkle glitter on the macaroni.

Interviewer: Do you sprinkle a lot of glitter on the macaroni?

Sydney: Yes, sprinkle a lot. After that, open the jar of paint and paint the can. Paint all around the can, but you don't have to paint the can completely. Finally, sprinkle some more glitter on the paint, and you are finished.

Interviewer: That's a beautiful pencil holder, Sydney. What will you do with it?

Sydney: I will give it to a friend. I won't sell it because people usually don't buy these pencil holders.

Interviewer: Why not?

Sydney: It is easy and fun to make these pencil holders, so people would rather make them than buy them.

Interpretation Check

A) What do you need to make a pencil holder? Fill in the blanks with the following words: pair, bag, jar, bottle.

1. You need a _____ of macaroni.

2. You need a _____ of glue.

3. You need a _____ of paint.

4. You need a _____ of glitter.

5. You need a _____ of scissors.

B) Circle the letter of the best answer to each question.

1. Where does Sydney pour the glue?

   a. She pours the glue under and inside the can.

   b. She pours the glue all over and around the can.

   c. She pours the glue on the top and on the bottom of the can.

2. What will happen if Sydney pours glue under the can?

   a. She will stick the can to the table.

   b. The glue will stick to the macaroni.

   c. She will need more macaroni.

3. How much macaroni does Sydney put on the can?

   a. She puts some pieces of macaroni on the can.

   b. She puts a little macaroni on the can.

   c. She puts many pieces of macaroni on the can.

4. How much glitter does Sydney sprinkle on the macaroni?

   a. She sprinkles a lot of glitter on the macaroni.

   b. She sprinkles a little glitter on the macaroni.

   c. She doesn't sprinkle any glitter on the macaroni.

5. Where does Sydney paint the can?

   a. She paints inside the can.

   b. She paints all around the can.

   c. She paints under the can.

6. What will Sydney do with the pencil holder?

   a. She will sell the pencil holder.

   b. She will keep the pencil holder.

   c. She will give the pencil holder to a friend.

Exercise D

Change the sentences you circled in Interpretation Check (B) to imperatives. Two sentences must have *you* as a subject. Other sentences don't need *you*.

1. _____
2. _____
3. _____
4. _____
5. _____
6. _____

Exercise E

Match the sentences on the left with the sentences on the right. Combine them with *because* or *and* or *so*.

1. You won't sell the pencil holder.

2. Sprinkle some more glitter on the paint.

3. It is easy and fun to make this kind of pencil holder.

4. Don't pour glue under the can.

a. You are finished.

b. People don't usually buy pencil holders.

c. You will stick the can to the table.

d. People would rather make them than buy them.

1. _____
2. _____
3. _____
4. _____

Exercise F: Summary

Tell how to make a pencil holder. Write three paragraphs. In your first paragraph, tell what things you need. Use the sentences you wrote in Interpretation Check (A) to help you write the first paragraph. In your second paragraph, tell what you do to make a pencil holder. In your third paragraph, tell what you will do with the pencil holder. Use the sentences you wrote in Exercises D and E to help you write the second and third paragraphs. These sentences need to be put in the correct order. What will the topic sentence of your first paragraph be?

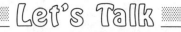

Pair Work: Christmas is a big national holiday in the U.S. It is on December 25th. For Christmas, many people make Christmas decorations to hang on their Christmas trees or to decorate their houses. The pictures below show how to make a Christmas tree decoration, but in Sequence A, the pictures are not in correct order. Sequence B is in correct order. You should describe Sequence B to a partner. Your partner should put numbers in the boxes in Sequence A. Then, you should switch tasks. The student who put numbers in Sequence A should now describe Sequence B to the other student. If you don't know how to say something, ask your teacher.

SEQUENCE A
How to Make a Christmas Decoration

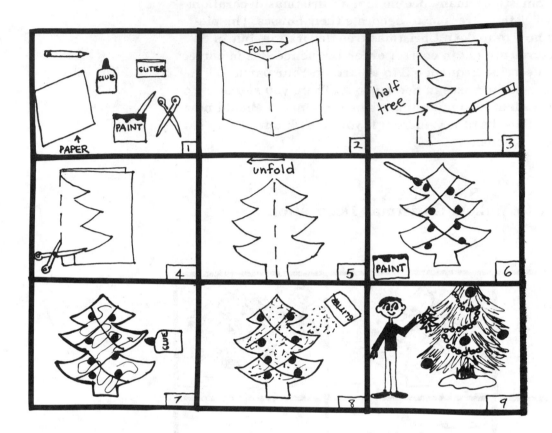

Exercise G

On a piece of notebook paper, write three paragraphs about "How to Make a Christmas Decoration." In your first paragraph, tell what things you need to make a Christmas decoration. In your second paragraph, tell what you do to make a Christmas decoration. In your third paragraph, tell what you will do with the Christmas decoration. Before you write, what is the topic sentence of your first paragraph?

HOW TO USE THE TELEPHONE

Exercise A

In small groups or pairs, read and discuss the sentences below. Are they true or false? If you don't know the answer, guess! Then read "How to Use the Telephone" and check your answers.

1. The yellow pages have advertisements and telephone numbers of shops and services. T F

2. Long distance costs twenty-five cents when you use a public telephone. T F

3. An area code has three numbers. T F

4. The country number for Japan is 82. T F

5. If you need help, you can dial 911, and the operator will send the police, the fire department or an ambulance. T F

6. If you don't know someone's telephone number, you can call 1-555-1212. T F

Reading (student composition)

How to Use the Telephone

If you are a foreign student in the U.S., the telephone might be difficult for you to use. You might not understand English well enough. You might not know how to find and call telephone numbers. I am a foreign student. I like to talk on the telephone, so I want to know how to use it.

If you don't know how to use the telephone, you can use the telephone book. There is a customer guide in the "white pages." The customer guide gives you special information such as how to find a telephone number, how to make long distance calls, and how to get telephone service. In the white pages, there is also a list of telephone numbers of the people in your area. The list is alphabetical by family name. The "yellow pages" of the telephone book have advertisements and telephone numbers of shops and services. For example, if you want the telephone number of a certain restaurant, look in the yellow pages under "restaurant." Then, look for the name of the restaurant you want to call.

You can use the telephone for local or for long distance calls. If you use a public telephone, local calls need only one quarter. However, when I called long distance to Los Angeles, I needed more quarters. I didn't know this. I was very surprised.

There are different area codes for long distance calls in the U.S. For example, Connecticut's area code is 203. If you call a number outside Connecticut, dial 1 + area code + local number. You can find area codes for everywhere in the U.S. in the customer guide of the telephone book.

Long distance international calling is very important for foreign students. When I came to the U.S. on the first day, I couldn't call Japan. I couldn't understand what the operator said. If you want to make a long distance international call, find your country number and routing or city code in the customer guide. For example, I live in Yokohama, Japan, so my routing code is 45, and my country code is 81. Then, dial 011 + country number + routing code + local number. You might need operator assistance.

Foreign students should also know the numbers to call for help or information. There are special numbers for public services in the customer guide. For example, the emergency number is 911. If you need the police, the fire department, or an ambulance, call this number. The directory assistance number is 1-555-1212. If you don't know someone's number, call directory assistance.

I tried long distance and international calls. My telephone bill was $117.00 last month. It was very expensive, but now I know how to use the telephone in the U.S. It is fun!

Minako Ojima, Japan

Interpretation Check

A) In "How to Use the Telephone," the writer combined many sentences with *if*. The sentences below are from the reading. Complete the sentences with the correct clause. Don't forget to put a comma in the middle of the two clauses when *if* is the first word in the sentence.

1. The telephone might be difficult for you to use _____.

2. If you don't know how to use the telephone _____.

3. _____ local calls need only one quarter.

4. If you call a number outside Connecticut _____.

5. Call directory assistance _____.

B) There are seven paragraphs in "How to Use the Telephone." What is the main idea of each paragraph? Circle the letter of the best answer.

1. 1st paragraph:
   a) foreign students in the United States
   b) the difficulty of the telephone for foreign students in the U.S.
   c) people like to talk on the telephone

2. 2nd paragraph:
   a) the telephone book
   b) the yellow pages
   c) the white pages

3. 3rd paragraph:
   a) long distance to Los Angeles
   b) local and long distance calls on a public telephone
   c) local calls

4. 4th paragraph:
   a) Connecticut's area code
   b) customer guide
   c) area codes

5. 5th paragraph:
   a) long distance international calls
   b) long distance to Yokohama, Japan
   c) country numbers

6. 6th paragraph:
   a) numbers for help or information
   b) emergency number
   c) directory assistance number

7. 7th paragraph
   a) how the writer feels about international calls
   b) how the writer feels about using the telephone
   c) how the writer feels about the telephone bill

Exercise B: Topic Sentences

When you look for the main idea of a paragraph in "How to Use the Telephone," you can find it in the first sentence of each paragraph. In this reading, the first sentence of each paragraph is a topic sentence. It gives the reader a general idea of what the paragraph is about. The paragraphs below are all about how to do something, but they don't have topic sentences. Read each paragraph, then circle the letter of the topic sentence that goes best with the paragraph.

1. First, boil water in a pan. Put a hot dog in the pan. Then, cover the pan and turn off the stove. Keep the hot dog in the pan for five minutes. Next, put the hot dog on a bun or a piece of bread. Finally, add mustard, pickles and onion.

    a. It is very difficult to make a hot dog.
    b. You can make a hot dog quickly.
    c. Hot dogs taste good with mustard.

2. You need a bucket of water, a mop, and a lot of soap. You also need a vacuum cleaner, a dust cloth, and a bottle of furniture polish. You should wear some old clothes or an apron because you don't want to get dirty. Now, you are ready to clean a house.

    a. You need a lot of things to clean a house.
    b. I don't like to clean houses.
    c. You need soap to clean a house.

3. First, ask the landlord how much the rent is. Then, ask if the rent includes electricity, gas or water. You should also ask if there is a deposit, laundry facilities and parking.

    a. Before you rent an apartment, you should talk to your friends about it.
    b. When you rent an apartment, you must ask about electricity and water.
    c. Here are some important questions to ask before you rent an apartment.

4. First, find the telephone number of a pizza place in the "yellow pages." Find a place that will deliver your pizza. Then, call the pizza place. Ask for a small, medium or large pizza and say what you want on the pizza, for example, mushrooms, olives or sausage. Finally, give your address. You will probably wait about thirty or forty minutes for your pizza to arrive.

    a. It is easy to order a pizza.
    b. Many Americans like pizza.
    c. It is fun to make pizza.

5. First, look at the front page and read the headlines. Then, look at the index to see what is inside, and find the section that interests you. For example, read section A to find international and national news. Read section B to find business news. Sections C and D have local and entertainment news. Section E has sports and classified advertisements.

    a. There is a lot of information in a typical American newspaper.
    b. The first section of an American newspaper has international news.
    c. American newspapers are confusing.

6. Drive north on the freeway. When you see the airport exit, turn right on the exit. Then, turn left at the first stoplight. Follow this road for three miles. You will see the airport parking lot on your left.
    a. There are many ways to get to the airport.
    b. If you want to go to the airport, follow these directions.
    c. Everyone loves to go to the airport.

Now, write a topic sentence for the next paragraph:

7. To make a scarf, you only need some balls of yarn and a pair of knitting needles. The yarn can be any color. The knitting needles can be large or small.

    topic sentence: _____

Exercise C

In "How to Use the Telephone," the writer supported her general statements with specific examples. She often used "for example" when she wanted to explain a general statement or give the reader more information. When you write, you will sometimes need to give examples so that your reader clearly understands you. You don't need to use "for example" every time you explain a general statement. Use it when you have a very specific fact or idea to add to your writing. The sentences below are from "How to Use the Telephone." Which are *general* statements and which are *specific* statements that give examples? Write G for general statements and S for specific statements.

1. The "yellow pages" of the telephone book have advertisements and telephone numbers of shops and services. _____

2. If you want the telephone number of a certain restaurant, look in the yellow pages under "restaurant." _____

3. There are different area codes for long distance calls in the U.S.

   _____

4. Connecticut's area code is 203. _____

5. If you want to make a long distance international call, find your country number and routing or city code in the customer guide.

   _____

6. I live in Yokohama, Japan, so my routing code is 45, and my country code is 81. _____

7. There are special numbers for public services in the customer guide.

   _____

8. The emergency number is 911. _____

Exercise D

Read the general statements below. What are some examples you could write to support these statements? When you write your example sentence, you can start the sentence with "for example." Remember to put a comma after the word "example." The first one is done for you.

1. I like American food.

   For example, I like hamburgers and hot dogs.

2. My country has many interesting customs.

_____

3. John plays soccer very well.

_____

4. I want to visit some of the national parks in the United States.

_____

5. English can be a difficult language to learn.

_____

Let's Talk

In small groups, fill in the chart below with the correct telephone numbers. You will need to look at a telephone book and the reading "How to Use the Telephone."

Information in the Telephone Book

country number and routing codes	area code	public service numbers	shops and services
Riyadh, Saudi Arabia	New York, New York	directory assistance	a Chinese restuarant
Tokyo, Japan	Mississippi	emergency	a bicycle shop
Mexico City, Mexico	Chicago, Illinois	telephone service	a movie theater
Jakarta, Indonesia	Connecticut	weather	a motel

Exercise E

On another piece of paper, write a paragraph. Discuss at least three kinds of information you can find in the telephone book. Where can you find the information? Give an example of each kind. Use the chart, "Information in the Telephone Book" to help organize your paragraph. Don't forget your topic sentence.

Discussion Questions

Talk about these questions in small groups or with a partner. Talking about these questions will give you more conversation practice. Also, you might get some good ideas for your next composition.

1. In the U.S., people make things for special holidays. For example, for Easter, people make Easter eggs. For Halloween, people make "jack o' lanterns." For Thanksgiving, people make a special turkey dinner. For Christmas, people make Christmas decorations and bake Christmas cookies. For St. Valentine's Day, people make valentines. (Maybe your teacher will show you how to do some of these things.) What special things do you make in your country for holidays?

2. What things do you know how to do? For example, can you cook something special? Can you sew or paint? Can you build or fix things? Explain how to do something to your group or partner.

3. What things did you need to know how to do when you came to the U.S.? What things do you want to know now? For example, do you know how to get a driver's license in the U.S.? Do you know how to get an airplane ticket? Do you know how to get telephone service?

Composition: Process Description

For your next composition, you can describe how to do something. Before you write your first draft, think about your topic. What things do you need? What do you do? How do you feel about what you make or what you do?

Exercise F: Pre-Writing

Sometimes it helps to make a list of vocabulary you will need to write your composition. Look at the examples below of vocabulary needed to write "How to Make a Pencil Holder," and "How to Use the Telephone." Then, try listing vocabulary you will need for your topic.

Topic: **How to Make a Pencil Holder**

vocabulary: can, macaroni, glue, glitter, paint
                pour, sprinkle, paint
                easy, fun

Topic: **How to Use the Telephone**

vocabulary: telephone book, white pages, yellow pages, customer guide
                local, long distance, area code, routing code, country number
                emergency, directory assistance
                expensive, fun

Your topic: _____

vocabulary: _____

                _____

                _____

Now, write the first draft of your composition. Use imperatives and
sequence words.

Revision

Before you turn in your composition, check it, or have a partner check
it. Use the questions below to help you. Talk to your teacher about your
composition after you have turned it in. Discuss what you wrote below.

1. Does each paragraph have a topic sentence? YES NO

   Write the topic sentence for each paragraph:

   _____

   _____

   _____

2. Do you give examples? YES NO

   Do you need to give more examples? YES NO

3. Do you use imperatives correctly? YES NO

4. Do you use sequence words correctly? YES NO

5. Do you combine sentences correctly? YES NO

6. Can you add a little more information on this topic?

_____

_____

7. What did you like or find interesting in this composition?

_____

_____

_____

5 Writing About the Future

In this chapter, we will talk about our predictions and plans for the future. First, we will discuss what might happen in the world in the future. Then we will discuss plans for a vacation around the world.

BY THE YEAR 2025

Exercise A

Discuss the vocabulary below. Then, look at the graphs. What problems will the world have by the year 2025?

environment	developed	increase	negative
pollution	developing	decrease	positive
population	Third World	technology	

WORLD POPULATION
(in billions)

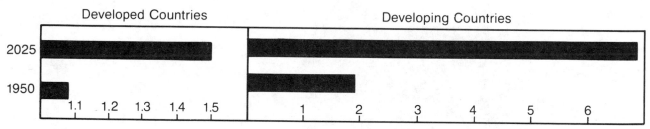

Developed Countries   Developing Countries

WORLD CARBON EMISSIONS
(in millions of metric tons)

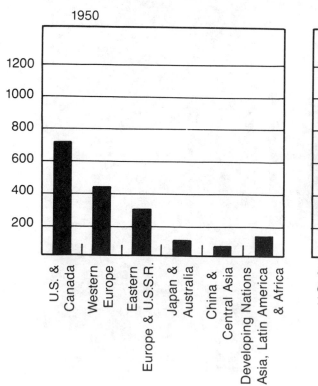
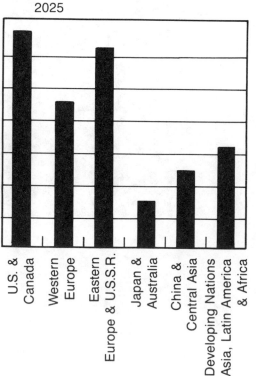

1950   2025

Future Tense

Future tense verbs are often formed by putting *will* before the simple verb. When you use *not* with a future tense verb, *will not = won't*. When you make a question, put *will* before the the subject.

Examples: You will be at home next week.   He won't go to New York.

You'll be at home next week.   Will he go to New York?

Will you be at home next week?

When will you be at home?

Note: You often use the prepositions, in and next when you use future tense, for example:

"In two days/weeks/months/years" and "next Friday/week/month/year".

Exercise B

Answer the questions below. You can look at the graphs to answer some of the questions, but other questions ask for your opinion: what do *you* think?

1. Where will population increase the most by the year 2025?

   _____

2. Which countries will cause the most carbon pollution in 2025?

   _____

3. Do you think the increase in population by 2025 will be more positive for the world or more negative?

   _____

4. How do you think countries will try to solve the pollution problem in the future? (You can write more than one sentence for this question.)

   _____

   _____

   _____

Exercise C

Combine the sentences below with the connecting word in parentheses.

1. By the year 2025, people will change. The environment will change. (and)

   _____

   _____

2. People will live longer. Population will increase all over the world. (because)

   _____

   _____

3. There is more pollution. There are more people. (so)

   _____

   _____

4. Changes that give people better lives are positive. Sometimes these changes are negative. (but)

   _____

   _____

Exercise D

Write one paragraph about "By the Year 2025." Use the sentences you wrote in Exercises B and C. Make sure your sentences are in correct order. Suggestion: the sentences in Exercise B are more specific, so they are good to use as examples of the general sentences in Exercise C. The first and last sentences are written for you. When you are finished, review this paragraph together on the board.

By the year 2025, people will change, and the environment will change.

   _____

   _____

   _____

   _____

   _____

Changes that give people better lives are positive, but sometimes these changes are negative.

Reading

By the Year 2025

In about twenty five years, the world will be a different place. People will change, and the environment will change. New ideas in science and medicine will definitely make some good changes, but will all changes be good?

Population is increasing very rapidly. By 2025, there will be over eight billion people in the world. Four billion of these people will live in Third World cities such as Nairobi and Mexico City. Because there will be so many people, we will probably change our lifestyles. There will be more jobs for "people services," such as medical and food services. People will live longer because there will be new medical discoveries. There will be less space for housing, so people will probably live in apartments or small houses. People will have fewer children, especially in developed countries. In Third World countries, industrial and technological developments will continue to affect people who are living very traditional lives. Maybe, there won't be any old, traditional societies still on the earth by the year 2025.

When people change, they change their environment too. For example, Brazil is becoming a more industrial country, so people are cutting down the rain forests of Brazil to make roads and build factories and dams. Every year, about 38,600 square miles of the world's rain forests are destroyed. If people don't control the loss of forests, there will probably be very few large rain forests by 2025. Pollution is also destroying forests. Industrial and automobile pollution have killed trees and poisoned lakes in large parts of the United States, Europe and Canada. Maybe, pollution from burning coal, oil and gas will change the earth's climate. Scientists are afraid that in fifty years, temperatures might increase as much as three degrees centigrade.

Changes that give people better lives are positive, but these changes sometimes cause other negative things to happen. For example, medicine helps people live longer, so there are more people who need housing and jobs. These people cut down forests for housing and jobs, but many plants we use for medicine come from the forests! Maybe, one of the greatest hopes we can have for the year 2025 is that we will increase communication and education so that changes are more positive than negative.

Interpretation Check

A) Read the second and third paragraphs of "By the Year 2025" again. Circle the letter of the main idea of each paragraph below. Then, write two details that go with each main idea. (There may be more than two details for each paragraph, but write only two.)

1. 2nd paragraph:
   a. Four billion people in Third World cities
   b. few traditional societies
   c. changes in population

   Details: _____

   _____

2. 3rd paragraph:
   a. few rain forests
   b. changes in environment
   c. warmer climate

   Details: _____

   _____

B) Look at the main ideas you circled and the details you wrote above. Write a topic sentence for each paragraph. (Don't look at the reading until *after* you write the sentences!)

1. topic sentence 2nd paragraph:

   _____

2. topic sentence 3rd paragraph:

   _____

Introductions and Conclusions

A good writer usually begins a composition with an introduction and ends a composition with a conclusion. In the readings in this textbook, the first paragraph is an introduction, and the last paragraph is a conclusion. An introduction is often short and general. It tells the reader what the main idea is of the **whole** composition. The conclusion is also often short and general. It often reminds the reader of the important points of the composition.

For example, in "By the Year 2025," the first paragraph tells you that the people of the world will change by the year 2025. It also tells you the environment of the world will change. These are the main ideas of the reading. In addition, the first paragraph says that maybe these changes will be good, and maybe they won't. In the last paragraph, you again read that changes are good and bad, and that these changes affect people and the environment. A conclusion is often very similar to an introduction, but it is not the same.

With your teacher, look at the first and last paragraphs of "National Parks in the U.S.," "American Espresso," and "How to Use the Telephone." These readings have the best examples of introductions and conclusions. How do the introductions give you a general idea of the whole composition? How do the conclusions remind you of the main points of the composition?

Exercise E

Change the sentences below by adding these words: _definitely, probably, maybe._ Do this without looking at the reading.

1. New ideas in science and medicine will make some good changes.

   _____

2. We will change our lifestyles.

   _____

3. People will live in apartments or small houses.

   _____

4. There won't be any old, traditional societies still on earth.

   _____

5. There will be very few large rain forests by 2025.

   _____

6. Pollution from burning coal, oil and gas will change the earth's climate.

   _____

Definitely	=	100% sure that something will happen	Definitely not	=	100% sure that something won't happen
Probably	=	80% sure that something will happen	Probably not	=	80% sure that something won't happen
Maybe	=	50% sure that something will happen	Maybe not	=	50% sure that something won't happen

Check the sentences you wrote in Exercise E with the reading "By the Year 2025." What are word order rules for using *definitely*, *probably* and *maybe?*

Note: *probably* and *definitely* come <u>before</u> *won't*. They can also come at the beginning of a sentence.

Summary

After the first reading in every chapter in this textbook, you are asked to do a *summary* exercise. A summary is a short version of a longer reading. A summary usually has the main ideas of a reading and a few important details. You don't usually need to use information from an introduction or a conclusion in your summary. Learning to summarize is always useful, and it is an especially important skill if you want to attend American universities.

Exercise F: Summary

Use the exercises in the Interpretation Check to write a two paragraph summary of "By the Year 2025." Use the topic sentences you wrote in Interpretation Check Exercise B for the beginning of each paragraph. Use the details you wrote in Interpretation Check Exercise A for the rest of each paragraph. You may also want to add a few sentences from Exercise E. Remember to indent each paragraph and to write complete sentences.

Read the statements below. What is your opinion? What do you think? Write *will* or *won't*, and *definitely, probably,* or *maybe,* in the column under "You." Talk to your partner. What does your partner think? Write *will* or *won't* and *definitely, probably,* or *maybe* in the column under "Your Partner." Tell your partner why you have your opinion. Try to give your partner an example or some details to explain your opinion.

IN 200 YEARS . . .

	You	Your Partner
1. Everyone speaks English.		
2. The earth is very polluted.		
3. The earth is very clean.		
4. There is a nuclear war.		
5. People visit other planets.		
6. People from other planets visit the earth.		
7. Some people have many children.		
8. People live under the ocean.		

Exercise G

On another piece of paper, write a paragraph about the future in 200 years. What is your opinion? Pick three statements above to write about, or think of three things you want to write about. Explain why you have your opinions. Give a few details or examples. Don't forget to write a topic sentence for your paragraph.

A DREAM VACATION

Exercise A

Your class has just won a trip around the world. The route is on the map below. Your trip begins in New York and ends in Taipei with seven stops in between. As a class, discuss your trip. (This discussion will be even more interesting if students or the teacher want to bring pictures to share.) Use the questions below to help your discussion.

1. Where are you going to go? What cities and countries are you going to see?

2. What will the weather be like in each country? What clothes are you going to bring?

3. What interesting customs will you learn about in each country?

4. What food are you going to try?

5. What special sights are you going to see?

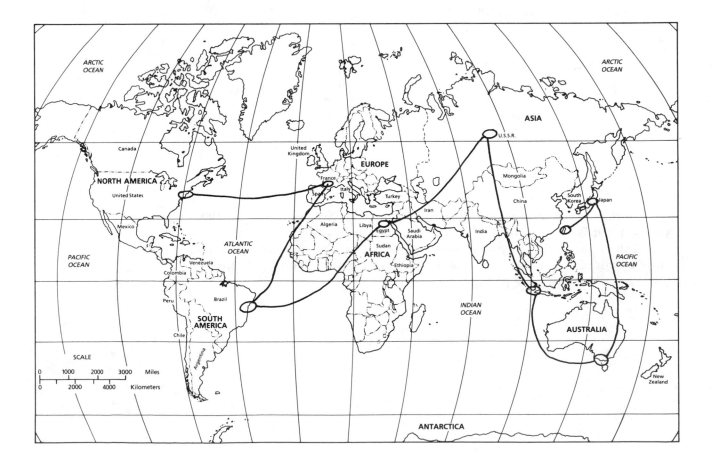

Future Tense

Future tense verbs are also formed by using a *be* verb + *going to* + simple verb. When you make a question, put the subject between the *be* verb and *going to*. The difference between *will* and *going to* isn't very important. People often use *going to* in speech when they are talking about plans.

Examples: He is going to visit Cairo in August.

               He's going to visit Cairo in August.

               Is he going to visit Cairo in August?

               When is he going to visit Cairo?

They aren't going to be in Paris next week.

Are they going to be in Paris next week?

Note: *going to* is often pronounced *gonna* in fast speech, but it is never written this way.

Exercise B

Fill in the blanks below with future tense. You can use *will* + simple verb, or use *be* + *going to* + simple verb. Use any simple verb that makes sense to you.

On my vacation, I _____ large cities. First, I

_____ to Paris. When I get to Paris, I

_____ croissants and drink coffee in sidewalk cafes.

Next, I _____ to Rio de Janeiro and Cairo. In Rio,

I _____ definitely _____ a bikini.

In the evening, I _____ in discothèques. In Cairo,

I _____ the Nile River. Then, I _____

Moscow, Jakarta and Melbourne. The weather _____

cold in Moscow, but it _____ hot in Jakarta and

Melbourne. Finally, I _____ to Tokyo and Taipei.

I _____ probably _____ sushi

when I am in Japan. I _____ glad to get to Taipei

because my family lives there.

Reading (student composition)

A Dream Vacation

When I go on my dream vacation, I am going to fly all over the world. I want to see what the world looks like. I am going to fly to Europe, South America, Africa, the Soviet Union, Indonesia, Australia, Japan and Taiwan. I am going to learn about different customs, try different food, and see different sights.

On my vacation, I will mainly see large cities. I will begin my trip in New York. Before I leave New York, I hope to see the Statue of Liberty and go to a Broadway play. Then, I am going to fly to Paris, France. In Paris, I will probably see the Eiffel Tower, the Louvre, and Notre Dame Cathedral. I am also going to sit in sidewalk cafes, eat croissants and drink coffee. I think this is a very popular custom in Paris.

Next, I will fly to Rio de Janeiro, Brazil and Cairo, Egypt. These cities are in warm, sunny climates, so I will shop for new clothes. In Rio, I will definitely buy a bikini and walk along the beautiful beaches. In the evening, I am going to dance in the discothèques. When I get to Cairo, I will see the Nile River. I also want to see the pyramids at Giza. Maybe I will try the delicious dates of Egypt.

After I visit Cairo, I am going to fly to Moscow in the Soviet Union. I want to see the communist way of life. I will see the huge building called the "Kremlin." The Soviet government is in this building. If I go to Moscow in the winter, the weather will be cold and snowy.

Then, I am going to fly to Jakarta, Indonesia and Melbourne in Australia. The weather in Jakarta might be very hot, humid and rainy, so I will definitely stay in the famous Mandarin Hotel. I want to be comfortable. While I am in Jakarta, I am going to eat a lot of food because Indonesian spices are so delicious. Maybe I will visit the island of Bali. I want to see the Hindu temples and watch the beautiful ceremonies and dances. After I visit Jakarta, I am going to fly to Melbourne, but I will probably only stay a few days in the city. I want to travel in the country and see the special animals. For example, I hope to see kangaroos and koala bears.

Finally, I am going to fly to Tokyo, Japan and Taipei, Taiwan. Tokyo is very expensive, so I might travel to other cities when I am in Japan. I hope to see the traditional city of Kyoto. Maybe, I will try on a kimono there. I will probably try sushi. My last stop will be Taipei because this is where my family lives. I won't travel anymore for awhile. I will be happy to be in a familiar place with familiar people.

In conclusion, my dream vacation will include some of the big cities of the world because I want to experience as much in life as possible. I want to understand the people of the world.

Juliana Kuo, Taiwan

Might & May

Might and *may* are **modals.** Modals are used with verbs, but they are not verbs. Modals come before the simple verb in a sentence. There are many modals, for example: should, can, could, must. Every modal has a certain meaning. *Might* and *may* mean possibility. Another way to say *might* or *may* is to use *maybe* and *will*.

> *Example:* Maybe I will go downtown tomorrow. = I might go downtown tomorrow.
> I may go downtown tomorrow.

Note: Modals often have more than one meaning. In this textbook, we will only discuss one meaning for each modal.

Interpretation Check

A) Read the statements below. If a statement is true, circle T, and write down a sentence from "A Dream Vacation" that shows the statement is true. If a statement is false, circle F and write down a sentence that shows the statement is false.

1. Juliana wants to see famous buildings on her vacation. T F

   _____

2. Juliana doesn't enjoy evening entertainment such as theaters and discotheques. T F

   _____

3. Juliana will probably buy a bikini in Rio de Janeiro. T F

   _____

4. The weather in Jakarta will definitely be hot, humid and rainy. T F

   _____

5. Maybe, Juliana will travel to other cities when she is in Japan. T F

   _____

6. Juliana will see only large cities on her vacation. T F

   _____

B) Circle the letter of the main idea of each paragraph.

1st paragraph: **a.** a trip around the world
(introduction) **b.** a trip to Europe
                    c. different food

2nd paragraph: **a.** New York and Paris
                    b. the Eiffel Tower
                    c. croissants

3rd paragraph: **a.** the Nile River
                    b. warm, sunny climates
                    c. Rio de Janeiro and Cairo

4th paragraph: **a.** the Soviet government
                    b. Moscow
                    c. cold weather

5th paragraph: **a.** Indonesian spices
                    b. Jakarta, Indonesia and Melbourne, Australia
                    c. kangaroos

6th paragraph: **a.** Tokyo, Japan and Taipei
                    b. sushi
                    c. familiar people

7th paragraph: **a.** big cities
(conclusion) **b.** people
                    c. experience through a trip around the world

Exercise C

Combine the sentences below to make one sentence. Use these connecting words: when, while, after, before, if, because, so, but. The sentences are from "A Dream Vacation," but you might be able to combine them differently and still be correct.

Note: Clauses beginning with *when, while, after, before,* and *if* usually stay in **present tense** when they are combined with a future tense clause.

Examples:

If I *study*, I will pass the test next week.   When John *sees* me again, I will be rich!
I will pass the test next week if I *study.*   I will be rich when John *sees* me again!

  1. I go on my dream vacation. I am going to fly all over the world.

_____

_____

2. I leave New York. I hope to see the Statue of Liberty.

_____

_____

3. I get to Cairo. I will see the Nile River.

_____

_____

4. I visit Cairo. I am going to fly to Moscow.

_____

_____

5. I go to Moscow in the winter. The weather will be cold.

_____

_____

6. The weather in Jakarta might be very hot. I will definitely stay in the Mandarin Hotel.

_____

_____

7. I am in Jakarta. I am going to eat a lot of food. Indonesian spices are so delicious.

_____

_____

8. I visit Jakarta. I am going to fly to Melbourne. I will probably only stay a few days in the city.

_____

_____

9. Tokyo is very expensive. I might travel to other cities. I am in Japan.

_____

_____

If you need to see more examples of sentence combining, look at "By the Year 2025" again. How many sentence are combined? How are they combined?

Exercise D: Topic Sentences

The paragraphs below are all about vacations, but the paragraphs don't have topic sentences. Read each paragraph and find the main idea. Then write a topic sentence on the line above the paragraph. Don't forget to indent the first word.

1. _____

We go there every summer. My little sister likes to go on the rides. My parents like to walk around. I like everything in Disneyland. I can't wait to go again this summer.

2. _____

When the weather is hot and sunny, I will probably stay on the beach. I will also visit Hawaii Volcanoes National Park, and watch traditional ceremonies and dances. If I go to a "luau," I want to try poi. In the evenings, I might go to the restaurants and theaters in Honolulu.

3. _____

Things are expensive in Paris, but she doesn't care. Susan especially likes to shop for clothes because Paris is the fashion capital of the world. She says the boutiques are much more fun to shop in than the big department stores in American shopping malls. Susan will probably go shopping in Paris again next year.

4. _____

He wants to see cathedrals in Europe, mosques in the Middle East and Buddhist temples in Asia. If he gets enough money, he will leave next fall. John hopes to write his thesis on religious buildings.

5. _____

There are good places to ski in Colorado. The weather is usually cold and clear on the mountains, and the snow is powdery, not wet. My friends and I will stay two weeks. I hope we can ski every day.

Pair Work: The two charts below show six American students' future plans. In pairs, you should look only at Chart A while your partner looks only at Chart B. Ask each other for the missing information in each chart, and write the information in your chart. Before you start, review with your teacher how to ask and answer future tense questions. Also, it will be helpful to review some of the vocabulary in the charts before you start.

KEY: will = no symbol   probably won't = X

will probably = ?   won't = XX

might = ??

CHART A
Plans for the Future

Sarah	go to college		get a degree in medicine ?		get married ??	
Jim		travel around ?		build his own house		have children ?
Sandy	go to college XX		be an actress ?		be a movie star X	
Mike		get an engineering degree		get a job overseas		have children ??
Karen	go to college ??		get married		have children ?	
Don		get a PhD in English ?		write a novel		have children XX

KEY: will = no symbol   probably won't = X

will probably = ?   won't = XX

might = ??

CHART B
Plans for the Future

Sarah		study chemistry		work in hospital ?		have children ??
Jim	work as a carpenter		start his own business		get married ??	
Sandy		go to New York		go to L.A. ??		be famous ??
Mike	go to college		travel around X	get married ?		
Karen		work in her father's company		buy a house		do community work ??
Don	go to college		teach in a university ?		get married X	

Exercise E

On another piece of paper, write a paragraph about your plans for your future. What are your plans for your education? a career? a family? Don't forget to begin with a topic sentence. You might also use sequence words: *first, then, next, after that.*

Discussion Questions

Talk about these questions in small groups or with a partner. Talking about these questions will give you more conversation practice. Also, you might get some good ideas for your next composition.

1. Is increase in population a problem in your country? Why or why not? Is pollution a problem? Why? If pollution is a problem, is your country trying to decrease pollution?

2. Do you think your country will change very much by 2025? Why?

3. Look at the map below and talk about a vacation you might take. Where will you go? What will you do and see?

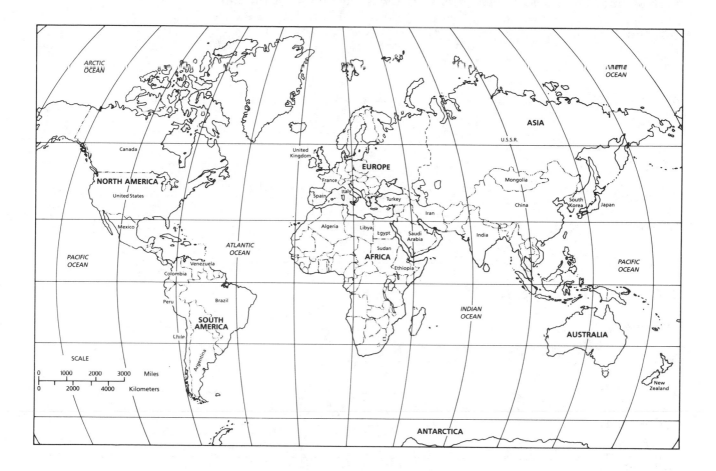

4. What are your plans for your future?

Composition: Writing About the Future

For your next composition, you can write about your opinion of the future of the earth and its people. You can also write about yourself: your plans for a vacation you want to take, or your plans for your life.

Exercise F: Pre-Writing

With your teacher, discuss possible main ideas and topic sentences for each sample topic below. Suggestion: After you decide what the topic sentences are, think about what you should put in your introduction and conclusion.

Topic: The Future of the World

introduction: _____

_____

2nd paragraph: _____

3rd paragraph: _____

conclusion: _____

_____

Topic: A Future Vacation

introduction: _____

_____

2nd paragraph: _____

3rd paragraph: _____

conclusion: _____

_____

Topic: My Future

introduction: _____

_____

2nd paragraph: _____

3rd paragraph: _____

conclusion: _____

Now, write the first draft of your composition. Pick a topic. Decide what your main ideas are.

Before you turn in your composition, check it, or have a partner check it. Use the questions below to help you. Talk to your teacher about your composition after you have turned it in. Discuss what you wrote below.

1. Does each paragraph have a topic sentence?   YES   NO

2. Does the composition have an introduction and a conclusion?   YES   NO

3. Do you use future tense correctly?   YES   NO

4. Do you use *definitely, probably, maybe, might* correctly?   YES   NO

5. Do you combine sentences correctly?   YES   NO

6. Do you give examples?   YES   NO
   Do you need to give more example?   YES   NO

7. Should you add more information? What questions do you have about this topic?

   _____

   _____

8. What did you like or find interesting in this composition?

   _____

   _____

6 Comparison and Contrast

A Comparison and Contrast composition describes the similarities and differences between people, places, things, ideas. In this chapter we will describe similarities and differences between Saudi Arabia and South Korea. Then, we will describe similarities and differences between people.

SOUTH KOREA AND SAUDI ARABIA

Exercise A

Look at the pictures of South Korea and Saudi Arabia. Then, read the sentences below and mark them true or false. If you mark a sentence false, change the sentence to make it true.

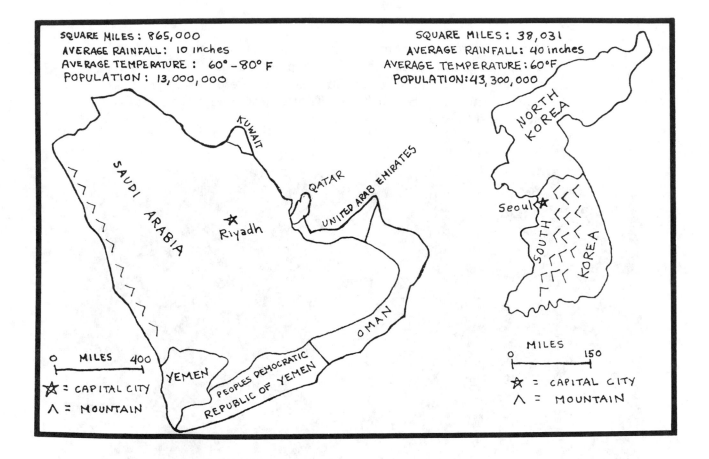

1. South Korea is bigger than Saudi Arabia.   T   F

_____

2. Saudi Arabia is drier than South Korea.   T   F

_____

3. South Korea is hotter than Saudi Arabia.   T   F

_____

4. Saudi Arabia is more mountainous than South Korea.   T   F

---

5. South Korea has a smaller population than Saudi Arabia.   T   F

Comparatives

When you want to describe differences between two people, places, things, ideas, you often use *comparative adjectives*. To form a comparative adjective, add *-er* to the end of the simple adjective, or put *more* before the simple adjective. You also use *than* after the adjective.

> *Examples:*   Tom is tall*er than* Bill.   Cars are *more* expensive *than* bicycles.
> Alaska is cold*er than* Florida.   Jane is *more* attractive *than* Carol.
> Writing is hard*er than* grammar.   My sister is *more* traditional *than* I.

Look at the examples above. Can you figure out when you use *-er* and when you use *more*?

The examples above all contained predicate adjectives, but the comparative rule is almost the same for adjectives that come before nouns. Remember to put *than* after the noun.

> *Examples:*   Alaska has a colder climate than Florida.
> Jack has darker hair than Don.
> Saudi Arabia has a smaller population than South Korea.

Can you change the examples above into comparative statements using predicate adjectives?

Spelling:

1. An adjective with one syllable, one consonant at the end of the syllable, and one vowel next to the consonant, doubles the final letter. For example, the final letter of these adjectives are all doubled: big, fat, thin, sad.

2. When an adjective with two syllables ends in *y*, drop the *y* and add *ier.* For example: happy, pretty, funny, easy.

Exercise B

Look at the maps of South Korea and Saudi Arabia again. Write one paragraph about the information in these maps. What will your topic sentence be?

_____

_____

_____

_____

_____

_____

_____

_____

Reading

South Korea and Saudi Arabia

South Korea and Saudi Arabia are countries that have a few similarities and many differences. There are similarities and differences in geography and climate, economy and government, and social customs.

The geography and climate in South Korea and Saudi Arabia are mostly different. Saudi Arabia is bigger than South Korea. Saudi Arabia has 865,000 square miles of land, and South Korea has 38,031 square miles of land. Saudi Arabia has a lot of desert, so the climate is often hot and dry. The average temperature in Saudi Arabia is between 60° and 80° Fahrenheit, and there are only 10 inches of rain a year. South Korea is more mountainous than Saudi Arabia. Also, South Korea's climate is cooler and rainier than Saudi Arabia's. The average temperature in South Korea is 60° Fahrenheit, and there are 40 inches of rain a year.

The economy and government in South Korea and Saudi Arabia are similar and different. The main products in South Korea are textiles and rice, but in Saudi Arabia, the main products are oil and dates. Jobs in South Korea are similar to jobs in Saudi Arabia. Both countries have many farmers and merchants. Also, jobs in South Korea are almost as industrial as jobs in Saudi Arabia. Twenty-nine percent of the people in Saudi Arabia work in industry. Twenty-five percent of the people in South Korea work in industry. The governments of these two countries are different. The government in South Korea is led by a president, but in Saudi Arabia, the government is led by a king.

Lifestyles and social customs are mostly different in each country. First of all, South Korea has a bigger population than Saudi Arabia. South Korea has about 43,300,000 people. Saudi Arabia has about 13,000,000 people. Because South Korea has so many people in a small area, people often live closely together. In Saudi Arabia, there is more space for fewer people. South Korea isn't as traditional as Saudi Arabia because the Saudi people follow the social laws of their religion, Islam, very closely. Religion is important in South Korea, but it isn't as important as it is in Saudi Arabia. In South Korea, people are Buddhist or Christian, and a few people are Confucian. Entertain-

BUDDHA

ment in South Korea is the same as entertainment in Saudi Arabia because people in both countries like to go shopping or go to restaurants.

South Korea and Saudi Arabia have different climates and geography, but these two countries are also different because Saudi Arabia is less developed than South Korea. The Saudi people are trying to develop their technology and to keep their Islamic traditions at the same time.

More Comparatives

When you want to describe differences between two things or people that are *less*, you use *less than* or *not as* simple adjective *as*.

Examples: Bill *isn't as* tall *as* Tom.   Bicycles are *less* expensive *than* cars.
Florida *isn't as* cold *as* Alaska.   Carol is *less* attractive *than* Jan.
Grammar *isn't as* hard *as* writing.   I am *less* traditional *than* my sister.

When do you use *less than* and when do you use *not as* simple adjective *as*?

Interpretation Check

A) Write the main idea of each paragraph.

1. 2nd paragraph: _____

2. 3rd paragraph: _____

3. 4th paragraph: _____

B) Circle the letter of the correct word or words.

1. The geography in South Korea and Saudi Arabia is ___.

   a. similar   b. different   c. the same

2. Saudi Arabia is ___ South Korea.

   a. bigger than   b. as big as   c. not as big as

3. South Korea is ___ Saudi Arabia.

   a. less mountainous than   b. more mountainous than
   c. as mountainous as

4. The main products in South Korea are textiles and rice, ___ in Saudi Arabia, the main products are oil and dates.

   a. so   b. because   c. but

5. Jobs in South Korea are ___ jobs in Saudi Arabia.

   a. the same as   b. different from   c. similar to

6. ___ countries have many farmers and merchants.

   a. similar   b. different   c. both

7. Jobs in South Korea are almost ___ jobs in Saudi Arabia.

   a. more industrial than   b. less industrial than   c. as industrial as

8. The government in South Korea is led by a president, ___ in Saudi Arabia, the government is led by a king.

   a. but   b. so   c. because

9. South Korea has a ___ population than Saudi Arabia.

   a. smaller   b. bigger   c. similar

10. South Korea is ___ Saudi Arabia.

    a. not as traditional as   b. as traditional as   c. more traditional than

11. Entertainment in South Korea is ___ entertainment in Saudi Arabia.

    a. different from   b. similar to   c. the same as

Words that Show Similarities and Words that Show Differences

When you describe two things or people, there might be many differences. To show differences and similarities, use the following words or phrases:

similarities	differences
both	simple adjective + -er than
be similar to/ be similar	more/less + simple adjective than
be the same as/be the same	be different from/ be different
be as simple adjective as	be not as simple adjective as

With your teacher, look through "South Korea and Saudi Arabia" again. Which sentences use words that show similarity? Which sentences use words that show difference? Put examples on the board of sentences using *similar to* and *similar, the same as* and *the same, different from* and *different.* Can you figure out the word order rule for using these expressions from the examples on the board?

Exercise C

Now, without looking at the text, write sentences about similarities and differences between South Korea and Saudi Arabia using the words below. The first one is done for you. Remember, the purpose of this exercise is to practice using words that show similarity and difference. There is often more than one way to express your meaning! Your sentences do not need to match the sentences in the text, but they need to be correct and true.

1. (big) _____

_____

2. (mountainous) _____

_____

3. (cool and rainy) _____

_____

4. (industrial jobs) _____

_____

5. (farmers and merchants) _____

_____

6. (government) _____

_____

7. (population and living space) _____

_____

8. (traditional) _____

_____

9. (religion) _____

_____

Exercise D: Summary

Write a three paragraph summary of "South Korea and Saudi Arabia."
Use the main ideas you wrote in the Interpretation Check to make topic
sentences for each paragraph. Use the sentences you wrote in Exercise
C to add details to each paragraph.

Exercise E: Paragraph Transformation

On another piece of paper, rewrite your summary using different main
ideas for your paragraphs. Write two paragraphs. The main idea of the
first paragraph can be only the *similarities* between South Korea and
Saudi Arabia. The main idea of the second paragraph can be only the
differences between South Korea and Saudi Arabia. This exercise would
work well if you work in pairs or small groups on one summary rewrite.
As a followup discussion, which summary do you like the most? Why?

You can bring a favorite music cassette to class. These tapes can be rock, classical, jazz, folk songs, etc. Play a song from two different tapes. Your classmates should listen and mark the chart below. You may need to play each song twice. Then, in small groups or pairs, you should compare your charts. Your teacher should put the chart on the board, poll the class, and reinforce grammatical structures used in showing similarity and difference. If you want to continue this activity, you can write the adjectives on another piece of paper and listen to more tapes. Before you start, do you understand the meaning of the adjectives?

Which Song Do You Like?

Key   similar/the same (=)   -er/more (>)   not as (adj.) as/less (<)

Name of song #1: _____

Name of song #2: _____

Adjectives	#1	#2
loud		
soft		
comforting		
exciting		
boring		
happy		
fast		
traditional		
modern		
romantic		

Exercise F

On another piece of paper, write a paragraph. Compare two songs. Which song do you like? Why? You don't need to use all the adjectives. Just use a few.

MY SISTERS AND I

Exercise A

Look at the physical characteristics and personality characteristics of the three sisters. Then, as a class, read the sentences below and mark them true or false. If you mark a sentence false, change the sentence to make it true on the board.

CATHY

age: 19
height: 5′5″
weight: 107 lbs.
brown eyes
short hair
traditional
creative
athletic
outgoing
easy going

MEG

age: 14
height: 5′7″
weight: 105 lbs.
green eyes
short hair
traditional
not creative
very athletic
shy
very serious

BARBARA

age: 15
height: 5′6″
weight: 100 lbs.
brown eyes
long hair
not traditional
very creative
athletic
very shy
serious

1. Barbara is older than Meg, but Barbara is younger than Cathy. Cathy is the oldest.   T   F

2. Cathy is taller than Meg, but Cathy is shorter than Barbara. Barbara is the tallest.   T   F

3. Cathy is heavier than Barbara and Meg. Meg is the lightest.   T   F

4. Cathy and Meg have brown eyes, but Barbara has green eyes.   T   F

5. Barbara's hair is as short as Cathy's. Meg's hair is the longest.   T   F

6. Both Cathy and Meg are traditional, but they are less traditional than Barbara.   T   F

7. Barbara is more creative than Cathy and Meg. Meg is the least creative. T F

8. Cathy is as athletic as Barbara. Meg is the least athletic.   T   F

9. Barbara isn't as shy as Meg. Cathy is less outgoing than Barbara. T F

10. Both Barbara and Meg are very serious. Cathy is the most easygoing. T F

Superlatives

When you want to compare more than two things or people, you will often use superlatives. To form a superlative adjective, add -*est* to the end of the simple adjective, or put *most* or *least* before the simple adjective. You also use *the* before *most* or the adjective with -*est*.

> *Examples:* Alaska is *the* cold*est* state in the U.S.
> My sister has *the* pretti*est* eyes in my family.
>
> Porsches are one of *the most* expensive cars.
> Grammar is *the least* difficult subject.

Note: good, bad and far are irregular adjectives: good–better–best
bad–worse–worst
far–farther–farthest

Spelling

The spelling rules are the same for superlative adjectives as they are for comparative adjectives.

When do you use -*est* and when do you use *most* or *least*?

Reading (student composition)
My Brothers and I

I have two brothers. The oldest brother is 28 years old. His name is Tetsumi. The other brother is 26 years old. His name is Masanobu. I am 24 years old, so I am the youngest. Also, I am the only daughter in my family. Although my brothers and I are close in age and have many things in common, we are also different in looks and personality.

My brothers and I have a few similarities and a few differences in physical appearance. For example, Tetsumi is as tall as Masanobu, but I am shorter than they are. Both Tetsumi and Masanobu have a strong build. I am smaller than they are, but I am more graceful. We all have dark hair and dark eyes, but my hair is longer than theirs.

In personality, my brothers and I also have a few similarities and a few differences. We all enjoy physical activity. Masanobu is the most active. He is always busy. Tetsumi is the most athletic. He is a good skier and has a ski instructor's license. I like to do aerobics and dance. My brothers have similar temperments. They are both outgoing and kind. I am shyer than they are, so they give advice to me about people and the world. They are very kind to me. They are probably the kindest brothers a sister could have.

I think the similarities and differences between my brothers and me are good. We learn from our differences, and our similarities help us to feel close to each other. My brothers live in Tokyo, and I live in the U.S., so I can't see them very often. I'm not lonely though. In my mind, I am always with them.

Yoshie Fujita, Japan

Outline

It is helpful to use an outline to organize the ideas of a reading after you read. You can also make an outline to organize ideas for a composition before you write. Usually, the main ideas have Roman numerals: I. II. III. IV. V. VI. VII. VIII. IX. X. etc. Specific ideas have capital letters: A. B. C. D. E. etc. More specific details have Arabic numbers: 1. 2. 3. 4. 5. etc. However, you can do an outline in different ways. Just remember to organize your ideas from most general to most specific.

Interpretation Check

The outline below is not complete. Finish the outline. What are the main ideas? What are the more specific ideas? What are the details?

My Brothers and I

I. Main Idea: (introduction) similarities and differences between brothers and sister

   A. ages:

      1. Tetsumi is 28

      2. _____

      3. Yoshie is 24

II. Main Idea: similarities and differences in physical appearance

   A. height:

      1. _____

      2. Yoshie is shorter

   B. _____

      1. Both Tetsumi and Masanobu have a strong build.

      2. _____

   C. hair and eyes

      1. _____

      2. _____

III. Main Idea: _____

   A. _____

      1. _____

      2. Tetsumi is the most athletic.

      3. _____

   B. temperament:

      1. _____

      2. _____

IV. Main Idea: (conclusion) similarities and differences are good

   A. They learn from each other.

   B. They feel close to each other.

Exercise B

On another piece of paper, rewrite "My Brothers and I." Use ONLY your outline for information and organization. Don't look at the reading! Your rewrite won't be the same as the reading, but it will be similar.

Exercise C

When you outline "My Brothers and I," you can see that each detail fits the main idea of each paragraph. In each paragraph below, there is a problem. There is one detail that DOESN'T fit the main idea of the paragraph. Read each paragraph and find the detail that doesn't fit. Draw a line through the sentence that has this detail.

1. I like American baseball more than American football. First, baseball is less violent than football. Baseball players don't tackle each other. Also, in baseball, you can see what players are doing more than you can in football. This is also true in soccer. Finally, if you live in a cold climate, it is more comfortable to watch baseball than football because baseball is played in the spring and summer, and football is played in the fall and winter.

2. For many students, community colleges are better than universities. Community colleges are cheaper, so students can afford tuition. Community colleges often offer more convenient class schedules for students who work part-time. When students work and take classes, they are usually very tired. Community colleges also offer more two-year programs for students who aren't as interested in an academic degree as students who attend universities.

3. The United States has many national parks. There are also many fine state parks. The largest national park is Wrangell-St. Elias in Alaska. This national park has the second highest mountain in the U.S. The smallest national park is Hot Springs in Arkansas. This park has forty-seven hot springs in an area of only nine square miles. Probably the most famous national park is Yellowstone. It has the world's largest geyser area.

4. Buying a new car can be difficult because there are so many styles to choose from. For example, a sports car such as a Porsche or a Corvette is probably more popular than a large sedan or small coupe because sports cars are usually the fastest and most fashionable cars. They are also the most expensive. American teenagers often buy used cars. Sedans can be similar to coupes in price, but coupes are sometimes more efficient in gas mileage. Large sedans are roomier and often safer than coupes and sports cars.

As a class, discuss the similarities and differences between the cars below. What is your opinion of each car? Include this vocabulary in your discussion: *powerful, luxurious, efficient* (gas mileage), *practical* (size and price), *sporty.* In pairs or small groups, talk about what type of car you might want to buy now. Then, talk about the type of car you might want to buy in the future. Use comparatives and superlatives to explain your choices.

Chevrolet Nova sedan $7,485

Honda Civic $7,551

Chevrolet Corvette convertible $38,728

Ford Aerostar wagon $12,295

Mazda sedan $21,629

Exercise D

On another piece of paper, write about cars. You can write about similarities and differences between cars, or you can write about a car you might want to buy now and a car you might want to buy in the future. Decide how many paragraphs you should write and what the main idea of each paragraph is.

Discussion Questions

Talk about these questions in small groups or with a partner. Talking about these questions will give you more conversation practice. Also, you might get some good ideas for your next composition.

1. Look at the LET'S TALK in Chapter 2 (page 32–33). Describe the similarities and differences between the same people in pictures A and B. For this activity, you will need to look at both pictures.

2. Use a current almanac to look up information about your country or a country you are interested in. Compare and contrast your country and other students' countries (You can find many kinds of almanacs in a bookstore or library, or your teacher can bring one or two almanacs to class. The "Countries of the World" section is very easy to use in an almanac.)

3. Talk about the similarities and differences in physical appearance and personality between you and your best friend or between you and other members of your family.

4. Think of some other topic you are interested in such as sports music, food, etc. Find another person who is interested in the same thing and compare and contrast types. For example, which do you like more, soccer or volleyball? Why? Which do you like more, American food or Chinese food? Why?

Composition: Comparison Contrast

For this composition, compare and contrast people or things. Pick a topic.

Exercise E: Pre-Writing

Write an outline below. You can use this form, or make your own. Try to follow your outline when you write. However, if you want to change your ideas while you write your composition, don't worry about following your outline.

Topic: _____

  I. Main Idea (introduction) _____

 II. Main Idea

    A. _____

    B. _____

    C. _____

III. Main Idea _____

    A. _____

    B. _____

    C. _____

 IV. Main Idea (conclusion) _____

Now, write the first draft of your composition. Use comparatives and superlatives. Use words for similarities and differences.

Before you turn in your composition, check it, or have a partner check it. Use the questions below to help you. Talk to your teacher about your composition after you have turned it in. Discuss what you wrote below.

1. Does each paragraph have a main idea?   Yes   No

   Write the main idea of each paragraph:

   _____

   _____

   _____

2. Do you use present tense correctly?   Yes   No

3. Do you use predicate adjectives correctly?   Yes   No

4. Do you use paragraph form?   Yes   No

5. Should you add more information?

   _____

   _____

6. What did you like or find interesting about this composition?

   _____

   _____

C H A P T E R

7 Narrative

A narrative is a real or imagined story. An imagined story isn't true. It comes from the writer's imagination. In this chapter, we will look at an old, traditional, Middle Eastern story, "Ali Baba and the Forty Thieves." This is an imagined story. Also, we will also look at a true story that a student wrote about an important time in his life.

ALI BABA AND THE FORTY THIEVES

Exercise A

Listen to your teacher read the story of Ali Baba. Follow the story by
looking at the pictures (scenes) below. Discuss the story with the scenes
a few times before doing Exercise B.

Past Tense

Past tense verbs are formed by adding -*d* or -*ed* to a regular verb or by changing an irregular verb. Use past tense when you want to talk about an event that began and ended in the past.

Examples:

Regular Verb	**Irregular Verb**
He walked to school yesterday.	He drank coffee yesterday.
Did he walk to school yesterday?	Did he drink coffee yesterday?
They walked to school yesterday.	They drank coffee yesterday.
When did they walk to school?	When did they drink coffee?

Use *didn't* with the simple verb when you want to use *not* in past tense:

He didn't walk to school yesterday.   They didn't drink coffee yesterday.

Past tense *be* verbs: *was, were*

Use *was* with I, he, she, it. Use *were* with you, we, they.

Examples:

I was happy yesterday.	They were in the house yesterday.
Were you happy yesterday?	Were they in the house yesterday?
Why were you happy yesterday?	Why were they in the house yesterday?

Note: a list of common irregular verbs and their past tense forms is in Appendix B.

Spelling

Add *d* when a verb ends in -*e* (danced). Add *ied* when a verb ends in -*y* after a consonant (studied). Double the final consonant and add -*ed* when a verb has one syllable, and one vowel followed by one consonant at the end of the verb (planned).

Exercise B

Look at the scenes below. Write a general sentence about each scene that explains the main point of the scene. Use past tense verbs.

_____

_____

_____

_____

_____

_____

_____

_____

_____

_____

_____

_____

_____

_____

_____

_____

_____

Exercise C: Summary

Put the sentences you wrote in Exercise B in correct story order. What happened first? then? etc. You may need to add more information so that your story makes sense. Write a sample summary on the board as a class.

_____

_____

_____

_____

_____

_____

_____

_____

_____

Reading

Ali Baba and the Forty Thieves

A long time ago, in a town in Persia, there were two brothers. Their names were Kasim and Ali Baba. Kasim married the daughter of a rich man, so Kasim and his wife were rich also. However, Ali Baba married a poor woman. He and his wife lived in a poor house, and Ali Baba sold wood to people in the town.

One day, while Ali Baba was cutting wood, he saw forty men on horses. They were riding toward him. Ali Baba thought these men were thieves, and he was afraid. He climbed a tree and watched the men. The men stopped at a place near Ali Baba's tree and took bags of gold and silver from their horses. The captain of the men walked up to a special spot at a rock cliff and said, "Open, oh sesame!" Suddenly, a large door opened in the rock. The thieves and their captain went in, and the door in the rock closed after them. Later, the door opened again, the men came out, and the captain said, "Close, oh sesame!"

After the men left, Ali Baba went to the rock and said the magic words, "Open, oh sesame!". The door opened and Ali Baba went in. He saw a huge cave filled with beautiful silk and carpets, and bags of silver and gold coins. Ali Baba took some of the bags and left the cave. He said the magic words, "Close, oh sesame!" and the door of the cave closed.

When Ali Baba went home, he showed the coins to his wife and told her about his adventure. "We must bury these coins so that no one will know our secret," he said. However, Kasim and his wife soon discovered the secret, and Ali Baba told Kasim the magic words. Kasim went to the cave and opened the door with the magic words, and the door closed after him. After he piled many bags of coins against the wall, Kasim said these words, "Open, oh barley!" The door stayed closed. Kasim said the names of many other grains, but he couldn't remember "sesame." While he was thinking, the thieves returned and killed him. They cut his body into pieces to warn anyone else who might come to the cave.

When Ali Baba came to the cavern to look for his brother, he found Kasim killed in this terrible way. Ali Baba took his brother's body home to bury. He asked Kasim's clever slave girl, Morgiana, to help him so that no one would know how Kasim died. Meanwhile, the captain of the thieves sent a man to find out who took Kasim's body. This man found Ali Baba's house and marked it with white chalk, but Morgiana discovered the chalk mark and marked all the other houses in the same way. When the captain came with his men, they didn't know which house was Ali Baba's. The captain sent another man to find and mark Ali Baba's house with red chalk, but again Morgiana marked all the other houses the same way.

Finally, the captain found Ali Baba's house himself and memorized its look. Then he brought all of his men back with him to kill Ali Baba, but the men hid in oil jars on mules so that Ali Baba wouldn't see them. The captain pretended to be an oil merchant and asked to stay at Ali Baba's house. Ali Baba didn't know that the oil merchant was the captain of the thieves. While the captain and Ali Baba were eating dinner, Morgiana discovered the thieves in the jars. The men thought she was the captain and asked her, "Is it time for us to come?" She said to each man, "Not yet, the time has not come." Then, she poured boiling oil into the jars and killed all of the thieves. Later, when the captain called his men to come and kill Ali Baba, he found them all dead. He was both angry and afraid, and as he was running away from Ali Baba's house, he swore to get revenge.

The captain tried one more time to kill Ali Baba. When he came to the town, he pretended to be a shop-keeper and called himself Khwajah Hasan. He became friends with Ali Baba's nephew. After some time, Ali Baba's nephew invited Khwajah Hasan to Ali Baba's house for dinner. Khwajah Hasan was very pleased and planned to kill Ali Baba after dinner, but the clever slave Morgiana, once again saved Ali Baba. She saw that Khwajah Hasan was really the captain of the thieves. She put on a dancing dress and hid a knife in the dress. Before the dinner was over, Morgiana entertained Ali Baba and the captain with her dance. When the captain reached in his purse to give money to Morgiana, she quickly killed him with her knife.

When Ali Baba realized Morgiana's courage, intelligence and loyalty, he was very grateful and said, "Allah be praised! You are free, and as reward I will marry you to my nephew!" No one else ever discovered Ali Baba's secret or his adventures with the captain and the thieves. Ali Baba taught his sons the magic words to the cavern, and his sons taught their sons. Therefore, Ali Baba's family lived happily for many, many years.

Interpretation Check

Work in pairs. Each of you should read a paragraph of "Ali Baba and the Forty Thieves" silently. Then, one of you should close the book and tell your partner everything you can remember about that paragraph. Your partner should check on this information by looking at the paragraph. Do this with each paragraph, but you should each do different paragraphs and take turns giving information.

Exercise D: Summary

On another piece of paper, answer the questions below. Write complete sentences. Write the answers to questions 1–4 in one paragraph. Write the answers to questions 5–9 in a second paragraph. Write the answers to questions 10–12 in a third paragraph. Write the answers to questions 13–15 in a fourth paragraph. Do this without looking at the reading.

1. What is the title of this story?

2. What is the setting (time and place) of the story?

3. Who are the main characters (most important people) in this story?

4. What are the relationships between these people?

5. What did Ali Baba see the captain of the thieves do?

6. What did Ali Baba do after that?

7. What did Ali Baba tell Kasim?

8. What did Kasim do then?

9. What did the thieves do to Kasim?

10. How did the captain try to kill Ali Baba? (Write two ways.)

11. How did Morgiana save Ali Baba? (Write two ways.)

12. Why was Ali Baba's family happy after that?

13. Who is your favorite character in this story? Why?

14. What lesson can people learn from this story? Why?

15. Why do you think this story is so loved and so famous?

Quotations

When you write what people say, you use commas (,) and quotation marks ("). In "Ali Baba and the Forty Thieves," the story is in past tense. However, the people in the story speak in different tenses. Look at the story again. How many quotations can you find? What is the punctuation of these quotations?

Exercise E: Rhetorical Transformation

Write dialog for the events that you wrote about in paragraphs 2 and 3. Do this as a class, in a group, or by yourself.

Scene 1: Ali Baba is in the tree. He is watching the thieves.

Ali Baba (to himself): _____

Captain (to his men): _____

Scene 2: Ali Baba is in the cave. He is looking at the bags of coins.

Ali Baba (to himself): _____

Scene 3: Ali Baba shows the coins to his wife. Then, Kasim and his wife enter.

Ali Baba (to his wife): _____

His wife: _____

Kasim: _____

Kasim's wife: _____

Ali Baba: _____

Scene 4: The captain kills Kasim in the cave.

Kasim (to the captain): _____

Captain: _____

Scene 5: In Ali Baba's house, Morgiana finds the thieves in the jars

Thieves: _____

Morgiana: _____

Scene 6: Morgiana kills the captain after she dances for him.

Captain: _____

Morgiana: _____

Ali Baba: _____

Let's Talk

Look at the picture below. With a partner or in small groups, make up a story about this picture. Who are the characters? What are their relationships? What is the setting? What happened? (plot) What is the title of your story? When you are ready, share your story with other groups.

Exercise F

Write your story on paper. Include the title, characters, setting and plot.

AN IMPORTANT TIME IN MY LIFE

Exercise A

In pairs, look at the scenes below and write two questions about each scene. Use past tense. Review the questions on the board as a class. Are they correct?

Scene 1: _____

_____

Scene 2: _____

_____

Scene 3: _____

_____

Scene 4: _____

_____

Exercise B: Summary

Pick eight of the best questions that you reviewed on the board, and write the answers to the questions. If you aren't sure what to write, guess! Use your imagination. Write in paragraph form. How many paragraphs should you write? Suggestion: Make up names or titles for the people in the pictures. Otherwise, your story will get confusing.

_____

_____

_____

_____

_____

_____

_____

_____

_____

_____

_____

Reading (student composition)

An Important Time in My Life

The first time I met Ahmed, my best friend, is both a sad and a good memory. One night in 1980, I was driving to a friend's house to have dinner. I saw a car behind me. I was driving fast, but this car was trying to pass me. Suddenly, another car came from the other direction. The driver of the car behind me couldn't get between my car and the car in front of me. Because we were driving fast, the accident happened. After that, I didn't know what happened.

When I woke up, I asked, "Where am I?" The doctor said, "You are in a hospital. Everything is okay." When I asked him about the driver of the passing car, the doctor said, "His name is Ahmed. He is in poor condition. I think he won't live until tomorrow night." I was very upset, and went to Ahmed's room. I was up all night with him. I felt I had known him for ages.

The next night, when I saw Ahmed, his health was better. The tears ran down my face. "Where is my cigarette?" he asked when he saw me. Then, he fell asleep again. His father was there and laughed at what Ahmed said because his father didn't know that Ahmed smoked.

From that time until now, Ahmed, my friend, is very close to me. I have great respect for him because he stood by me in all my troubles.

Sami Al-Sadhan, Saudi Arabia

Interpretation Check

Write an outline of "An Important Time in My Life." Use the form below. The main ideas are written for you.

I. *The first time Sami met Ahmed is a sad and a good memory.* _____

   A. _____

   B. _____

II. *Sami was in the hospital with Ahmed.* _____

   A. _____

   B. _____

III. *Ahmed was better the next night.* _____

   A. _____

   B. _____

IV. _____

Exercise C

Put the events below in time order by writing a number next to the event. What happened first? second? third? etc. Don't look at the reading until after you try to put the events in order.

___ Ahmed fell asleep again.   ___ Sami saw a car behind him.

___ The accident happened.   ___ The tears ran down Sami's face.

___ Ahmed asked for a cigarette.   ___ Sami was driving to a friend's house.

___ Sami woke up.   ___ Sami went to Ahmed's room.

___ Ahmed's father laughed.   ___ Another car came from the other direction.

___ Ahmed and Sami became friends.   ___ The doctor told Sami about Ahmed.

Exercise D

Sentence combining: Combine the sentences below using *when* or *after*.

1. Sami didn't know what happened. The accident happened.

_____

2. Sami asked the doctor about Ahmed. The doctor told Sami about Ahmed.

_____

3. Sami saw Ahmed. Ahmed's health was better.

_____

4. Ahmed asked for a cigarette. Ahmed saw Sami.

_____

Pronoun Reference

In the sentences above, you can change the second noun in the sentence to a pronoun if the first and second nouns are the same; for example, "Ahmed asked for a cigarette when he saw Sami." However, you must be careful when you use pronouns. If you write: " "Sami saw Ahmed when his health was better," it isn't clear whose health was better: Sami's or Ahmed's.

Exercise E

Read the sentences below. Are the pronoun references clear? If not, replace the pronoun with the name that goes with the pronoun. You don't need to replace every pronoun!

1. When Sami asked the doctor about Ahmed, he told him about him.

2. After Ahmed asked Sami for a cigarette, he fell asleep again.

3. Ahmed's father laughed at what he said because he didn't know that he smoked.

Exercise F

Sometimes, the pronoun reference isn't clear if you only read one sentence, but the reference is clear if you read the sentences before or after a sentence. Read "An Important Time in My Life" again below. Some of the pronouns have been taken out. Write the pronouns.

The first time I met Ahmed, my best friend, is both a sad and a good memory. One night in 1980, _____ was driving to a friend's house to have dinner. I saw a car behind _____. I was driving fast, but this car was trying to pass _____. Suddenly, another car came from the other direction. The driver of the car behind _____ couldn't get between _____ car and the car in front of _____. Because _____ were driving fast, the accident happened. After that, _____ didn't know what happened.

When I woke up, _____ asked, "Where am _____?" The doctor said, "_____ are in a hospital. Everything is okay." When _____ asked _____ about the driver of the passing car, the doctor said, "_____ name is Ahmed. _____ is in poor condition. I think _____ won't live until tomorrow night." I was very upset, and went to Ahmed's room. _____ was up all night with _____. I felt I had known _____ for ages.

The next night, when _____ saw Ahmed, _____ health was better. The tears ran down _____ face. "Where is _____ cigarette?" _____ asked when _____ saw _____. Then _____ fell asleep again. _____ father was there and laughed at what Ahmed said because _____ father didn't know that Ahmed smoked.

From that time until now, Ahmed, my friend, is very close to _____. _____ have great respect for _____ because _____ stood by _____ in all _____ troubles.

Past Continuous Tense

Past continuous verbs are formed by adding *-ing* to the end of the simple verb. You also need to put a past tense *be* verb before the simple verb. You don't need to use past continuous tense very often. Use it when you want to talk about an action that happened at a specific time in the past: My brother was taking a final exam yesterday at 3:00. (He began to take the exam sometime before 3:00 and continued to take the exam after 3:00.) Also, use past continuous when you want to talk about two actions that happened in the past. One action happened first and then was stopped by or continued after the second action. In this case, two sentences are often combined using *when, while, as*: While my brother was taking a final exam yesterday, he got very sick.

> *Examples:* You were reading all morning yesterday.
> Were you reading all morning yesterday?
> When I saw her, she was sitting in the restaurant.
> Where was she when you saw her?

Exercise G

Read "Ali Baba and the Forty Thieves" again. There are five examples of past continuous tense in this story. Can you find them? Write them down. How are they used?

1. _____

2. _____

3. _____

4. _____

5. _____

Read "An Important Time in My Life" again. Can you find examples of past continuous tense? How are they used?

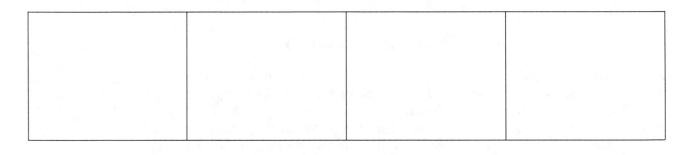

Let's Talk

Think of four important memories in your life. They can be good or bad. In the boxes below, write only the setting (time and place) of your memory and the names of the people in your memory. Don't write anything else. When you are finished, show your memory boxes to a partner and tell the story of each memory. Then, find a new partner.

Exercise H

Write about two or three of your partners' memories. You can write about different partners. Write at least two paragraphs.

Discussion Questions

Talk about these questions in small groups or with a partner. Talking about these questions will give you more conversation practice. Also, you might get some good ideas for your next composition

1. Can you remember the first time you traveled to a foreign country? What was your first day like? What sights, sounds and smells do you remember? What was the weather like? What surprised you? What disappointed you? What frightened you? What excited you? What was the best and the worst thing that happened that day?

2. What is the strangest thing that happened to you? Or, what is the funniest thing that happened? Add a lot of details!

3. Tell an old story from your culture. Think of stories you learned in school or stories your parents told you when you were a child. Think of old folktales, fairy tales, or ghost stories.

4. Tell the story of your favorite movie, book or play.

Composition: Narrative

For this composition, write about a story or a memory that is very special to you. Before you write your first draft, do some *pre-writing:* put some of your ideas on paper by making an outline, or making a list of vocabulary and ideas, or drawing pictures or scenes. In this composition, it is very important to add a lot of interesting details. If you write about a memory, think about what you saw, heard and felt. Think about what people said. If you write a story, you must imagine these details.

Revision

Before you turn in your composition, check it, or have a partner check it. Use the questions below to help you. Talk to your teacher about your composition after you have turned it in. Discuss what you wrote below.

1. Is the composition well-organized? (in good order)   YES   NO

2. Does the composition have setting and characters?   YES   NO

3. Do you use past tense and past continuous tense correctly?   YES   NO

4. Do you use quotations correctly?   YES   NO

5. Do you combine sentences correctly?   YES   NO

6. Do you need to give more examples or details?   YES   NO

7. Should you add more information?

_____

_____

8. What did you like or find interesting in this composition?

_____

_____

8 Advice and Opinion

When you tell people what you think they should do, you are giving them advice. When you tell people what you think or believe, you are giving your opinion. Your advice and opinions are usually based on your personal feelings. In this chapter, we will look at a foreign student's advice to other foreign students living in the U.S. Then we will look at one student's opinion of an important world problem, the use of nuclear arms.

ADVICE TO STUDENTS

Exercise A

As a class, discuss these questions: How can foreign students get along in the United States? How can you make friends? How can you find a comfortable place to live? How can you find entertainment? How can you best learn English?

Exercise B

Read the sentences below and fill in the blanks with these modals: should, shouldn't, must, mustn't, can, can't. More than one answer can be correct. What are you able to do? What is your opinion?

1. Students _____ make American friends.

2. Students _____ meet Americans in dorms or in conversation groups.

3. Students _____ join college activities.

4. Students _____ join intramural sports, outdoor clubs and craft and music organizations.

5. Students _____ live alone.

6. Students _____ live with a friend in an apartment, in a dorm, or with a host family.

7. Students _____ practice English only in the classroom.

8. Students _____ use English with each other, with American students, and with the people in the community.

Should & Must

Should and *must* are *modals*. Modals are used with verbs, but they are not verbs. Modals come before the simple verb in a sentence. Every modal has a certain meaning. *Must* has a very strong meaning: an action is *necessary*. You *have no choice*. *Should* isn't as strong as *must*. *Should* means an action is *a good idea*. You *have a choice*. When you make a question with a modal, put the modal before the subject.

> *Examples:* People must eat or they will die.
> Must people eat?
> People should exercise because it is good for their health.
> Why should people exercise?
> People shouldn't drink a lot of coffee.
> Should people drink a lot of coffee?
> Why shouldn't people drink a lot of coffee?

Another way to say *must* is *have to* or *has to.*

> *Examples:* People *have to* eat.   John *has to* take medicine everyday.
> *Do* people *have to* eat?   *Does* John *have to* take medicine everyday?

Note: *had better* has a stronger meaning than *should,* but isn't as strong as *must.*

Exercise C

Look at the sentences you completed in Exercise B. Make questions.

1. (y/n) _____

2. (Wh) _____

3. (y/n) _____

4. (Wh) _____

5. (y/n) _____

6. (Wh) _____

7. (y/n) _____

8. (Wh) _____

Exercise D

Write an interview. Pick four questions from the ones you wrote in Exercise C. Then, write the answers to the questions. Write your own answers. You can use the sentences in Exercise B to help you. Begin with this question:

Question: How can foreign students get along in the United States?

Answer: _____

Question: _____

Answer: _____

Question: _____

Answer: _____

Question: _____

Answer: _____

Question: _____

Answer: _____

Reading

Advice to Students

You will read an interview in which Juan Martinez gives advice to foreign students. Juan is a Mexican student who has studied languages in the U.S., Brazil, and France.

Interviewer: How can foreign students get along in the United States?

Juan: First, it's important to be as open and flexible about the new culture as possible. Students should make American friends. This will help students understand American culture. Also, American friends can help students manage problems of housing, transportation, banking, and so on.

Interviewer: It is easy to say students should make American friends, but this can be very difficult. How can students meet Americans?

Juan: Of course, if students live on the campus of an American university, they can meet Americans in dormitories. However, sometimes dormitories aren't available, or they are too expensive, so another way to meet Americans is to find conversation groups or partners.

Interviewer: How can students do this?

Juan: Sometimes, English language programs do this for foreign students. Students can also do this themselves by putting a note on the bulletin board in the Student Center that asks for conversation partners. There are many American students, especially those in International Studies, who want to talk to foreign students. In addition, there are many American students who are studying foreign languages. They may want to practice their language skills with a

STUDENT CENTER BULLETIN BOARD

foreign student. For example, if a Spanish student practices English with an American student who is studying Spanish, the American student can then practice Spanish with the Spanish student.

Interviewer: How can a foreign student find such an American student?

Juan: A foreign student can ask the teacher of a language class to make an announcement to the class. Or, again, the foreign student can put a note on the student center bulletin board.

Interviewer: What else should students do to make friends?

Juan: The best way to make friends, whether you are foreign or not, is to join activities such as intramural sports, outdoor clubs, music and arts programs, or special non-credit classes.

Interviewer: How can students do this?

Juan: They should check the bulletin board in the student center for flyers that announce meetings and times. Also, students should go to the offices where these activities are organized. Usually, student centers have special offices for these activities where students can get information and sign up for activities.

Interviewer: You mentioned that sometimes dormitories aren't available or are too expensive. What should students do for housing?

Juan: Well, if possible, they shouldn't live alone. This can make living in a foreign country even more difficult and lonely. Foreign students should live with an American host family or with a friend in an apartment. English language programs often arrange host families for foreign students. Also, living with a host family is a great way to practice English!

Interviewer: In conclusion, what advice can you give concerning the best way for a foreign student to learn English?

Juan: Students shouldn't practice English only in the classroom. They must use English with each other, with American students, and with the people in the community. This will give students an "English brain." The best way to learn a language is to use it all of the time. Using English all of the time can be difficult to do, but it is definitely worth it.

Interpretation Check

Look at the statements below. Some are general ideas and some are specific details which support the general ideas. Write G next to the general statements and S next to the specific statements. There are three general statements and seven specific statements.

1. They should join activities such as intramural sports, outdoor clubs, music and arts programs, or special non-credit classes. ____

2. Students should make American friends. ____

3. They can meet Americans in dormitories. ____

4. Then, they will have an "English brain." ___

5. They can find conversation groups or partners. ___

6. They should live with an American host family or with a friend in an apartment. ___

7. The best way for students to learn a language is to use it all of the time. ___

8. Students shouldn't live alone. ___

9. Living with a host family is a great way to practice English. ___

10. They must use English with each other, with American students, and with the people in the community. ___

Exercise E: Summary

Put the statements above into paragraph order. Write three paragraphs. The general statements are the topic sentences of each paragraph.

Exercise F: Rhetorical Transformation

On another piece of paper, write a letter to a friend in your country. Give your friend advice on how to get along in the U.S. You can use the ideas and details in the reading, but please use some of your own ideas and details.

Let's Talk

Advice Column: Write a problem on an index card. The problem can be a world problem or a personal problem. For example: "I have a problem. My roommate says she must sleep with the windows open every night. I get very cold. What should I do?" Don't write your name. Your teacher will collect your cards and write the problems on the board. In pairs or small groups, take turns giving advice about each problem.

Exercise G

Pick two or three problems you want to write about. Give advice about these problems. On another piece of paper, write at least two paragraphs.

NUCLEAR ARMS

Exercise A

Look at the graphs below. The pie graph shows how the United States government spends the money in its budget. Figure out the percentage of each section of the pie graph. For example, what percentage does the U.S. spend on national defense? What percentage does the U.S. spend on education and social services? What is your opinion of this budget? The line graph shows how terrorism incidents involving nuclear weapons have increased or decreased in different areas of the world from 1966 to 1985. Where did most of these incidents happen? What do you think the reasons for these incidents were?

Budget of the U.S. Government
(in billions)

Total Budget Expenses: 1,004.6 billion dollars

* includes: Agriculture 27.4
Education & Social Services 29.7
Transportation 26.2
Health 40.0
Veterans Benefits 26.8
etc.

INTEREST

OTHER*

INCOME SECURITY

138.6   214.8

123.2

282.0   DEFENSE

SOCIAL SECURITY & MEDICARE

282.4

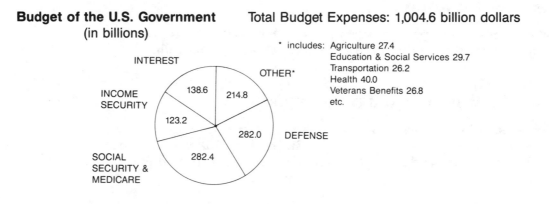

Nuclear Related Terrorist Incidents

Vocabulary

national budget: the amount of money the government of a country receives and spends

national defense: the armies, weapons, machines, research, etc. that a government develops to protect and defend the country in a war.

gross national product (GNP): The value of all goods and services that a country bought in one year

terrorism incidents: Acts of violence done usually by political groups in a country against other groups in the country, or against other countries.

Exercise B

Write answers to the questions below. Even if you disagree with the question, try to think of general reasons.

Why should a country have nuclear arms? Write two general reasons.

1. _____

   _____

2. _____

   _____

Why shouldn't a country have nuclear arms? Write two general reasons.

3. _____

   _____

4. _____

   _____

Exercise C

Write an example that supports each reason you wrote above. Use the information in the graphs to help you:

reason #1: A country should have nuclear arms because many countries of the world have them, and a country without nuclear arms has no protection.

example #1: Terrorist incidents happened in countries in Asia, Africa, Europe, North and Latin America, and the Middle East.

example #2: _____

_____

example #3: _____

_____

example #4: _____

_____

Exercise D

As a class, review the reasons and examples your classmates have thought of. Then, write a paragraph about your opinion. Do you think countries should have nuclear arms? What are your reasons? What examples support your reasons? Begin your paragraph with a good topic sentence.

_____

_____

_____

_____

_____

_____

_____

_____

Reading (student composition)

Nuclear Arms

Many countries in this world have nuclear arms. These nuclear arms can destroy the world more than three times over. Governments in these countries say they use nuclear arms only for protection. However, if nuclear arms can destroy the world three times, what is there to protect?

Some people are for nuclear arms. They say countries should have nuclear arms for protection. For example, when the Soviet Union invaded Afghanistan in 1980, many of the Afghani soldiers only had 100 year old rifles to fight with. The people of Afghanistan couldn't defend themselves. They had to buy modern weapons. Some people in Western Europe think the U.S.S.R. will invade Western Europe if the countries of Western Europe don't have nuclear arms. Some Western Europeans worry that Eastern Europe will increase its nuclear weapons technology more quickly than Western Europe.

People who are against nuclear arms say that instead of giving money to nuclear weapons, governments must give money to social projects in their countries and in Third World countries. Japan spends less than one percent of its GNP on weapons, and Japan has a very good economy. On the other hand, in 1987, the United States used twenty-seven percent of its budget on national defense and only fourteen percent on health and human services. This includes education! I think many countries now use around fifteen percent or more of their GNP for their armies each year. Many people question if fifteen percent is enough for protection, but is this only for protection? I think many governments want to sell their weapons to other countries for profit. In 1984, world arms imports cost thirty-five billion dollars. However, world grain imports cost only thirty-three billion dollars!

In conclusion, I can understand both sides of this problem. People need protection from invading armies, but governments must spend too much money on defense, and sometimes this money isn't only for "defense." I feel the governments in this world must find a compromise for the problem. To find this will be very difficult, and the people of the world will need a long time to do it.

Andrey Oei, Germany

Interpretation Check

Read the statements below. Circle T if they are true, and circle F if they are false. Then, copy sentences from the reading that show the statements are true or false.

1. The main idea of the second paragraph is why people are against nuclear arms.   T   F

   _____

2. Andrey gives one reason why people are for nuclear arms.   T   F

   _____

3. Andrey gives two examples of parts of the world where people say countries should have nuclear arms for protection.   T   F

   _____

   _____

4. A reason why people are against nuclear arms is because there are better ways to spend all of the money that is spent on weapons.   T   F

   _____

5. Andrey says Japan is an example of a country that has a strong economy because its government spends a lot of money on weapons.   T   F

   _____

6. The U.S. is an example of a country that spends fifteen percent of its national budget on defense.   T   F

   _____

7. In the introduction, there are two sentences that give a general idea of opinions for and against nuclear arms.   T   F

   _____

   _____

8. In the conclusion, Andrey says he is against nuclear arms.   T   F

   _____

Exercise E

Fact or Opinion? Statements of fact give information that everyone agrees is true. Statements of opinion give information that someone *thinks* is true. Not everyone agrees with statements of opinion. Often, statements of opinion have words like: *People say* or *I think* or *I feel.* Also, the words *should* and *must* are often used in opinion statements. The statements below are from the reading. Are they statements of fact or statements of opinion? Write *fact* or *opinion* next to each sentence. If you aren't sure, look at the reading again and read the complete statement.

1. Many countries in this world have nuclear arms. _____

2. Countries should have nuclear arms for protection. _____

3. The U.S.S.R. will invade Western Europe if the countries of Western Europe don't have nuclear arms. _____

4. Governments must give money to social projects. _____

5. Japan spends less than one percent of its GNP on weapons.

_____

6. In 1987, the United States used twenty-seven percent of its budget on national defense. _____

7. I think many governments want to sell their weapons to other countries for profit. _____

8. In 1984, world arms imports cost thirty-five billion dollars. _____

9. I feel the governments in this world must find a compromise for the problem. _____

More Modals

There are past tense forms for some modals. The modal *can* means ability. The past tense form for this is *could*. *Have to* means necessity. The past tense form for this is *had to*.

> *Examples:* I *couldn't* speak English very well a year ago, but I *can* now.
>
> You *have to* take a test to get your driver's license. I *had to* take my test when I was sixteen.

Note: The negative form of *have to* and *had to* do not mean necessity. They mean there is or was choice in an action.

> *Examples:* I don't *have to* exercise every day, but I enjoy running, so I run two miles a day.
>
> I didn't *have to* study English when I was in school in my country, but I wanted to.

Exercise F

The sentences below are from the reading. Fill in the blank with the modal you think fits. Although the reading has a certain modal for each sentence, there may be more than one modal that fits without a big change in meaning. Don't look at the reading until after you finish.

1. Nuclear arms _____ destroy the world more than three times.

2. People say countries _____ have nuclear arms for protection.

3. The people of Afghanistan _____ defend themselves. They

   _____ buy modern weapons.

4. Governments _____ give money to social projects in their countries.

5. Governments _____ find a compromise for the problem.

Reference

The word *this* is very useful when you are writing English. You can use it to refer to a word or phrase you wrote in a previous sentence or clause. For example, in the third paragraph of "Nuclear Arms," Andrey writes:

"On the other hand, in 1987, the United States used twenty-seven percent of its budget on national defense and only fourteen percent on health and human services. *This* includes education!" What does *this* refer to?

Here is another sentence from the third paragraph:

"Many people question if fifteen percent is enough for protection, but is *this* only for protection?" What does *this* refer to?

Exercise G

The sentences below are from the reading, "Advice to Students." Circle the letter of the phrase that *this* refers to.

1. Students should make American friends. This will help students understand American culture.
   a. making American friends
   b. understanding American culture

2. Another way to meet Americans is to find conversation groups or partners. Sometimes, English language programs do this for foreign students.
   a. meet Americans
   b. find conversation groups or partners

3. The best way to make friends is to join activities such as intramural sports, outdoor clubs, music and arts programs, or special non-credit classes. How can students do this?
   a. join activities
   b. make friends

4. Students shouldn't live alone. This can make living in a foreign country even more difficult and lonely.
   a. living alone
   b. living in a foreign country

5. Students must use English with each other, with American students, and with the people in the community. This will give students an "English brain."
   a. using English with each other
   b. using English with everybody

Read the statements below. Talk to a partner. What is your opinion?
Write a modal under "YOU." What is your partner's opinion? Write the
modal that expresses your partner's opinion under "YOUR PARTNER."
Use *should, shouldn't, must, mustn't, don't/doesn't have to.* Then ask each
other the reasons for your opinions. Try to give examples or specific details to support your reasons.

OPINION SURVEY

	You	Your Partner
1. Everyone ___ get married.		
2. People ___ marry for love.		
3. People ___ let their parents arrange their marriages.		
4. People ___ have children. (if they can)		
5. A woman ___ work if she has children.		
6. A man ___ work if he has children.		
7. People ___ get divorced if they have children.		

Exercise H

As a class, review all of your classmates' opinions. How do most of your classmates feel about each statement? What are their reasons? What are some examples to support their reasons? Then, write at least two paragraphs about your classmates' opinions and the reasons for their opinions. How do they feel about marriage? How do they feel about children?

Discussion Questions

Talk about these questions in small groups or with a partner. Talking about these questions will give you more conversation practice. Also, you might get some good ideas for your next composition.

1. Did people give you advice before you came to the U.S.? What did they say?

2. What advice about life in general (education, work, love, etc.) would you give to a person younger than yourself? What advice about life did you get when you were younger?

3. What is your opinion of American food? Why? For example? Do you think everyone agrees with your opinion? Why? For example? What is your opinion of golf? Why? For example? Do you think everyone agrees with your opinion? Why? For example? What is your opinion of the Rambo movies? Why? For example? Do you think everyone agrees with your opinion? Why? For example?

4. What do you think is the biggest problem in the world today? What is your opinion of this problem? Why? What is another opinion of this problem? Why?

Composition: Opinion

For this composition, you can write about a problem in society, or about a kind of food, music, art, sport, etc. You will need to write about two opinions. In your introduction, give a general idea of both opinions of your topic. You may write as many paragraphs about each opinion as you can. Please give reasons for each opinion, and a few examples of the reasons. In your conclusion, you should give your opinion, or if you agree or disagree with both opinions, say so, and give a reason for your feelings.

Exercise I: Pre-Writing

Below, is an example of Andrey's pre-writing. The general ideas are in big circles. The more specific reasons and examples are in smaller circles. Try to do this with your composition before you write it.

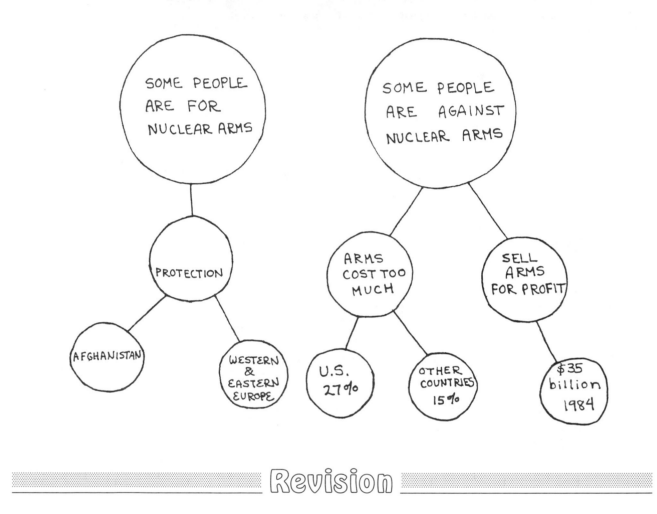

=========================== Revision ===========================

Before you turn in your composition, check it, or have a partner check it. Use the questions below to help you. Talk to your teacher about your composition after you have turned it in. Discuss what you wrote below.

1. Is the composition well-organized? (in good order) YES NO

2. Does the introduction generally discuss both opinions of the topic? YES NO

3. How many paragraphs are there for each opinion?

4. Does each opinion have at least one reason and one example? YES NO

5. Do you need to give more reasons or examples? YES NO

6. Does the conclusion give your opinion of the topic? YES NO

7. Do you use modals correctly? YES NO

8. What ideas or details could you add to this composition?

_____

_____

9. What did you like or find interesting in this composition?

_____

_____

9 Synthesis

In this text, you have used different kinds of organization for your compositions: biography, description, process description, comparison and contrast, narrative, opinion. However, a composition can have more than one form of organization. In this chapter, we will read about housing in the U.S. and about changes in lifestyle in Japan. We will write about these topics using different forms of organization. When you combine more than one form of organization in a composition, you synthesize forms.

RENTING

Exercise A

Look at the pictures below. These buildings have different kinds of
architecture: modern, Colonial, Victorian and Ranch Style. Describe the
buildings. What are they made of? How many floors (stories) do they
have? Are they traditional or modern? Are they attractive? ugly? boring?
interesting? Which building do you like? Why?

Exercise B

Read the rental advertisements for each building. Discuss the vocabulary and the abbreviations. What good points does each rental place have? Are there any bad points? Would you rent these places? What do these words mean: condition, utilities, appliances, studio, duplex, highrise, deposit, furnished, porch.

Note: this exercise will be more relevant and interesting if you use current ads from area newspapers.

A FANTASTIC VIEW!!
• Studio, 1&2 Bdrms from $320
• UTILITIES INCLUDED
• Locked entrance
• Covered parking available
• Gracious adult living
• Scenic historic neighborhood

854-1322

KING TOWER
901 SW KING

COLONIAL home in exc cond, 2BR, 2BA, 10 mins to city, very quiet street-Westmoreland, lrg yard. W&D, refrig, nice deck & porch.

$450 + dep. 628-7201

COZY UP in a 2 bdrm duplex w/fireplace, $430 OR 2 bdrm townhouse, 1½ baths, $375. On busline. Powell Park Estates, 3154 SE 136,

858-1167 Princeton Prop Mgmt

IT'S AN OLDIE
But Lovely & Roomy
4+ BEDROOM-Victorian, 1618 SE Clinton St, $550. 254-8290. Grocery, drug store, city park & bank 1–2 blocks away. Ideal for downtown employee.
1st & last, damage & cleaning dep. required.

Exercise C

The sentences below are topic sentences from six paragraphs of the reading, "Renting." Before you look at the reading, use the ideas and vocabulary from the pictures and from Exercise B to write one detail sentence under each topic sentence.

1. Many apartment buildings in the U.S. are modern high-rises or multi-story buildings.

_____

_____

2. An alternative to these apartments are duplexes, or large houses that have been divided into apartments.

_____

_____

3. People often rent whole houses.

_____

_____

4. How do people find these places?

_____

_____

5. Next, you should make an appointment with the landlord in order to look at the place and maybe to fill out an application form.

_____

_____

6. Finally, if you decide you want to rent the place, and the landlord accepts you as a renter, you must sign a rental agreement.

_____

_____

Exercise D

Now, write a short introduction and conclusion to go with these sentences. What general things can you say about renting?

introduction: _____

_____

_____

conclusion: _____

_____

_____

Reading

Renting

Finding a place to live in the United States can be a big job. Style, condition, cost, location, and availability of rental places are the important things to consider when you look for an apartment or a rental house.

Many apartment buildings in the U.S. are modern high-rises or multi-story buildings. These buildings offer different types of apartments such as studios, one-bedroom and two-bedroom apartments. They may be furnished or unfurnished. A positive point about these buildings is that there are building managers who are supposed to repair and maintain the apartments. The apartments are supposed to be clean and ready for you when you move in. A negative point is that the buildings and apartments often have a boring style. People who live in these apartments might feel like they are living in little white, cement boxes that all look the same.

An alternative to these apartments are duplexes, or large houses that have been divided into apartments. Duplexes are two apartments joined side by side or one on top of the other. They may have a modern or a traditional style. Or, they may be two parts of an old house. Often, old houses are more interesting to live in because of their architectural style. On the East Coast, many old houses have Colonial architecture dating from the 1700s. These two-story houses are often made of brick and have rows of windows across the face of the house. There may be a metal eagle over the front door and a small porch. On the West Coast, the old houses have mainly wooden Victorian architecture from the 1850s. These two-story houses have high ceilings, large windows, and a lot of decoration. A negative point about renting apartments in old houses is that the plumbing and heating are usually old also, and they need repair.

People often rent whole houses. A young married couple or a small family may rent a house until they save enough money to buy a house. Also, groups of students often rent a house and divide the rooms among themselves. A typical rental house for these people has a ranch style architecture. This style became popular in the 1950s and 1960s. These houses are usually economical and easy to repair, but some people think they aren't very interesting. Ranch houses are usually one-story rectangular buildings with small narrow windows.

How do people find these places? First, the most common way is to look in the rental advertisements in the newspaper. If you are living in a big city, rental places probably are listed by location: northeast, southwest, etc. You can also call a rental agency. These agencies help people find rentals according to cost and location. However, if you use a rental agency, you must pay a fee. Also, you can just walk or drive around an area where you want to live. Sometimes, there are signs that say "For Rent" in front of a building or house.

Next, you should make an appointment with the landlord in order to look at the place and maybe to fill out an application form. When you go to the place, look at everything: plumbing, electrical outlets, appliances, windows, doors, floors, walls and ceilings. Then, ask a lot of questions: Are pets allowed? Can you lock the doors and windows securely? Is there a parking space? Are you near stores, bus stops, and laundromats? How much do utilities (water, heat, electricity, garbage) cost? Do you have to pay the first and the last months' rent? Is there a cleaning fee?

Finally, if you decide you want to rent the place, and the landlord accepts you as a renter, you must sign a rental agreement. These papers give many details about what the renter is responsible for and what the landlord is responsible for. It is very important to read and understand everything in this agreement before you sign your name. If you don't understand something, you must ask the landlord.

Of course, getting what you want in the location you want can be very difficult. This is especially difficult in the larger cities of the U.S. such as New York, Washington D.C., Chicago and San Francisco. Rent is very expensive, and many good places are not available. In this case, what do people do? They keep trying! Sooner or later, the almost-perfect-place will become available.

Interpretation Check

A. Match the building with the description:

1. ranch house   ____ multi-story cement boxes, modern

2. Victorian house   ____ rows of windows, a small porch, a metal eagle, 1700s

3. duplex   ____ one-story rectangular buildings, narrow windows, 1950s

4. Colonial house   ____ two apartments joined side by side or one on top of the other

5. high-rise apartments   ____ wooden houses, a lot of decoration, high ceilings, 1850s

B. Put the steps in order. What do you do first? second? third?

Ask a lot of questions. ____

Look in the advertisements,
call a rental agency, or drive around an area and look for signs. ____

Sign a rental agreement. ____

Make an appointment with the landlord. ____

Look at everything in the place. ____

Read and understand everything in the agreement. ____

Rhetorical Organization

In this text, you have used description, process, comparison and contrast, narrative, and opinion organizations. A description composition tells where things and people are, and what they look like. A process composition tells how to do something. A comparison and contrast composition describes similarities and differences between things or people. A narrative composition tells a story. An opinion composition explains at least two opinions of a topic. A composition can have more than one form of organization. In the reading, "Renting," there are two main forms of organization. What are they? Which paragraphs show these forms?

Exercise E

You can sometimes change compositions or parts of compositions from one organization to another. For example, paragraphs two, three and four give you descriptions of five kinds of buildings, but you can also compare and contrast these buildings. Write sentences and use the adjectives in parentheses to compare and contrast these buildings.

1. (modern) _____

   _____

2. (traditional) _____

   _____

3. (interesting) _____

   _____

4. (big) _____

   _____

5. (economical) _____

   _____

6. (narrow) _____

   _____

Exercise F

The process part of "Renting" (paragraphs 5, 6 and 7) can be changed to narrative. You must change the imperative verbs to past tense. Read this shortened version of paragraphs 5, 6 and 7. Then, rewrite it as a narrative. Use past tense and the pronoun "I."

How do people find a place? First, look in the rental advertisements in the newspaper. Next, make an appointment with the landlord in order to look at the place and to fill out an application form. When you go to the place, look at everything. Finally, when you decide you want to rent the place, and the landlord accepts you as a renter, you must sign a rental agreement.

_____

_____

_____

_____

_____

_____

_____

Exercise G

On another piece of paper, write three paragraphs. Compare and contrast the place you are living in now and the place you lived in before you came to the U.S. Then, write your opinion. Which place do you like? Why? Finally, tell how you found the place you live in now. Who did you talk to? How much does it cost? etc.

Describe Picture A to your partner. Your partner will draw the things
and people you describe in the empty square below Picture B. Then
your partner will describe Picture B, and you will draw the picture in
the empty square below Picture A. Before you begin, review count/non-
count nouns and articles. When you are finished, talk about the differences and the similarities between these pictures.

PICTURE A

PICTURE B

Exercise H

Write a one paragraph description of one of the pictures above. What is
the picture of? Is this place modern or traditional? How much or how
many things do you see? Where are they? What are the people doing?

CHANGES IN JAPANESE LIFE

Exercise A

For most of the people of the world, the twentieth century has brought many big changes in their ways of life. Think about the people in your own country as they were one hundred years ago and as they are now. How did they change? As a class, talk about the questions below. Compare the past and the present.

1. What kind of work did children do 100 years ago? How much did they work? What do they do now? What did children play 100 years ago? Where did they play? How much did they play? Now?

2. How many people lived in one home 100 years ago? What were their relationships? Were they formal? strict? What happened when children grew up and got married? Where did they and their families live? Were grandparents important members of the family? Why? Now?

3. Who did the work in the home (cooking, cleaning etc.) 100 years ago? How much work needed to be done in the home? Was it easy or difficult? Why? Now?

4. What kinds of jobs did people have 100 years ago? About how much money did they make? Were the jobs usually in offices? factories? farms? Who did these jobs? Now?

5. What did people do for entertainment 100 years ago? Where did they go? What did they eat? How much money did they spend? How much free time did they have? Now?

Melvin & Ernestine Jones and children
Ohio, 1929

Reading (student composition)

Changes in Japanese Life

Now, everything is moving fast in Japan. People are walking fast. There are a lot of instant foods. Fashions for women's clothes change very fast. People can have a comfortable life because of technology. However, people lost their simple and traditional life. As a result, there are big changes in the lifestyle of the family, especially children, and the lifestyle of Japanese society in general.

Ten years ago, there was still some vacant land in Tokyo. Children could play baseball or play house there. In suburban areas, children went to rice fields to catch crawfish or dragonflies. My brother and I did this. In fields, there were many horsetails or berries, and people picked them to eat.

In contrast, children of today can't find spaces for play. They might find an open space, but it probably isn't natural ground. It is a concrete space. Furthermore, children sometimes don't know how to play outside well because a family computer is very popular among children in Japan. After school, children go back to their homes as soon as possible so that they can play computer games.

DRAGONFLY

Families had to change in Japan. In the past, people lived with their grandparents. All of the family respected the old people. Young people obeyed the old people and listened to their advice. Sometimes the relationship between the young people and the old people was difficult because the relationship was stricter and more formal than it is now.

Now, most Japanese people have a nuclear family. Only the parents and the children live together in one home. Usually people don't have more than two or three children. As a result, people can think about the life of the individual. They don't have to take care of so many people in their families. Now, some old people live alone because they don't want to be a burden upon their families. Children in a nuclear family can live in their own way. For example, they don't have to worry about how much cake they can eat with their sisters or brothers at tea time!

My family is a nuclear family, but my grandmother lives with us. My grandmother is very modern. She likes to watch T V shows that are very popular with young people, and she likes to try everything. I always ask her when I have problems, and she gives me good advice. My grandmother taught my mother and me how to make Japanese traditional food. However, my family couldn't do activities like long trips because of my grandmother. We had to choose a special place when we made a plan to go somewhere. I think people should be considerate of the feelings of old people.

Finally, there are important changes in the everyday activities of society. In the past, people made a fire for cooking, and people had to do everything by themselves. However, now, people can get everything they want when they just push a button or turn on a switch. Life changed from a hand-made style to an automatic style. These days, people can't live without technology, and the use of automatic machines is increasing. On the other hand, people are now paying money to experience the simple life. In Japan, mineral water shops are very popular, so people go to a shop to just drink water. There are other silly shops in Tokyo. There are air bars. People just breathe fresh air from air pumps. People spend money to get things that should be free.

In conclusion, I don't know if the changes in Japan are good or bad. People can't go back to the old life, but young people should try to understand old customs and tradition, and old people should try to understand the new culture. People are not going to grow if they don't know how old people built the society. However, it is also important to accept the positive changes in society and work to improve negative changes. I think people are like music makers. People gather to live like musical notes in a measure. There are many kinds of notes, and they get together to make a harmony. We have to help each other.

MUSIC MEASURES

Rie Suzuki, Japan

Interpretation Check

Read the sentences below. If they are true, circle T. If they are false, circle F and write a TRUE sentence.

1. Many years ago, everything was moving fast in Japan.   T   F

_____

2. There is still some vacant land in Tokyo.   T   F

_____

3. Maybe, children will find an open space in Tokyo.   T   F

_____

4. Families didn't have to change in Japan.   T   F

_____

5. People usually have more than two or three children. T F

_____

6. Rie never asks her grandmother about her problems. T F

_____

7. In Tokyo, people spend money to get things that must be free. T F

_____

8. People won't grow if they know how old people built the society. T F

_____

9. Rie thinks people must help each other. T F

_____

Exercise B

Write two sentences about each question:

What did people do every day in your country 100 years ago?

_____

_____

What do the people do every day in your country at present?

_____

_____

What are people or the government in your country doing now to improve people's lives?

_____

_____

What do you think the future of the people of your country will be like?

_____

_____

Transition Words

Some words in English are like the sentence combining words, *but, and, so.* These words are often at the beginning of sentences, and they connect with the ideas in the sentences before them. *In contrast, on the other hand,* and *however* are transition words that are similar to *but.* They show difference. *Furthermore* is similar to *and.* It shows addition. *As a result* is similar to *so.* It shows cause and effect. You don't need to use transition words in every sentence. A difference between the sentence combining words *but, and, so* and transition words is punctuation. Often, transition words go at the beginning of a sentence and have a comma. Sentence combining words *but, and, so* go in the middle of two clauses and have a comma.

Exercise C

Read the paragraphs below. Write the transition words or the sentence combining words that you think fit. Use *and, but, so,* or *furthermore, however, in contrast, as a result.*

People can have a comfortable life because of technology.

_____, people lost their simple and traditional life.

_____, there are big changes in the lifestyle of the

family, especially children. Ten years ago, there was still some vacant

land in Tokyo. In fields, there were many horsetails or berries,

_____ people picked them to eat.

_____, children of today can't find spaces for play.

Children today might find an open space, _____ it

probably isn't natural ground. It is concrete space.

_____, children sometimes don't know how to play out-

side well because a family computer is very popular among children in

Japan. After school, children go back to their homes so that they can

play computer games.

Exercise D

The rhetorical organization of "Changes in Japanese Life" is comparison and contrast. Rie mainly describes differences between Japanese life in the past and in the present. Rie's introduction is very good. The details in the beginning of the introduction are interesting. The last sentence of the introduction makes a general statement about the important points of the composition: "There are big changes in the lifestyle of the family, especially children, and the lifestyle of Japanese society in general." Now, the reader knows what the composition is about and in what order the main ideas will be given. Each paragraph has a main idea, but the most general points of the composition are: changes in children's and family life, changes in the life of the society.

Put the sentences below in outline order. There is more than one way to do an outline, but if you need guidance, use the following frame for the sentences.

My family

Now, no more natural ground

Before, people lived with their grandparents

Changed from hand-made style to automatic style

Before, Tokyo had vacant land

Changes in life of Japanese children and families

My grandmother gives me good advice

Old and young people should try to understand each other

Changes in everyday activities of society

Now only parents and the children live together in one home

Children played baseball

People must pay money for simple things

Relationship was stricter

Opinion of changes

Children play computer games

Air bars and water shops

People think about individual life

I. _____

   A. _____

      1. _____

   B. _____

      1. _____

   C. _____

      1. _____

   D. _____

      1. _____

   E. _____

      1. _____

II. _____

   A. _____

   B. _____

      1. _____

III. (conclusion) _____

   A. _____

In groups of three, look at the statistics about American women in terms of marriages and divorces, college graduates, and working population. Each student should pick one topic and make a graph showing the changes from past to present. Compare your graphs to the graphs in other groups. Then, talk about these questions: Because of these changes in the lives of American women, what do you think are positive and negative changes in the lives of American children? What do you think are positive and negative changes in the lives of American families? What do you think are positive and negative changes in American society?

Marriages & Divorces

	Marriages	Divorces
1900	709,000	55,751
1950	1,667,231	385,144
1987	2,421,000	1,157,000

College Graduates

	Men	Women
1900	22,173	5,237
1950	328,841	103,217
1987	480,000	498,000

Working Population

	% of working women out of total women	% of working women out of total working population
1900	18.8	18.3
1950	33.9	29.0
1987	56.1	44.3

Exercise E

Write about the facts in the statistics above. Then, write what you think about these facts. Give your opinion of changes in the life of American women. Do you think they are positive? negative? Write two or three paragraphs.

Discussion Questions

Talk about these questions in small groups or with a partner. Talking about these questions will give you more conversation practice. Also, you might get some good ideas for your next composition.

1. Think about a beautiful home that you want to live in. What is your "dream" house? Draw a plan of this house. Describe it to your partners. What will the house be made of? What will the style be? Where will the rooms be? What will be in them? How many people will live there? Will you have pets? What will the outside look like (trees, gardens, sports places, etc.)?

2. What are some similarities and differences between traditional buildings and modern buildings in your country?

3. Do you have a nuclear family or an extended family? Was your childhood very different from your parents' or your grandparents' childhoods? Why?

4. How will you raise your children? Will you be strict and formal? Will you teach the same things to your daughters and sons? What activities will you do with your son? What activities will you do with your daughter?

Composition: Synthesis

For this composition, you can mix (synthesize) organizational forms, or choose one form you like. You can also choose your own topic. You have written about many topics in this class. Is there a topic you haven't written about that you are interested in? Is there a topic that you have written about that you would like to write about again?

Exercise F: Pre-Writing

Look at all of the writing, compositions and paragraphs, that you have done for this class. Look at the different organization and topics. Then, think about a new or an old topic. Discuss it with your teacher. Decide on the organization.

Before you turn in your composition, check it, or have a partner check it. Use the questions below to help you. Talk to your teacher about your composition after you have turned it in. Discuss what you wrote below.

1. How is the composition organized?

2. Does the introduction make a general statement about the important points of the composition?   YES   NO

3. Do you need to give more details, reasons, examples?   YES   NO

4. Is there a conclusion?   YES   NO

5. What ideas or details could you add to this composition?

   _____

   _____

6. What did you like or find interesting in this composition?

   _____

   _____

APPENDIX A

Grammar & Writing

Pre/Post Test

A. Circle the best answer.

1. There are ___ oranges in the fruit bowl. (much, any, a little, many)

2. While I ___ watching TV last night, the electricity went off.
   (be, was, is am)

3. I need your advice. ___ I exercise more often? (have to, might, should, will)

4. The man is sitting ___ the table. (at, in, between, in back)

5. Where ___ you going to go on vacation? (do, be, are, will)

6. Jane is ___ than Sally. (richer, tallest, good, small)

7. Right now, I ___ a test. (took, am taking, was taking, will take)

8. There ___ any food. (won't, aren't, weren't, isn't)

9. My sweater was dirty ___ I dropped it. (but, because, while, if)

10. My mother often ___ dinner. (cooks, is cooking, cook, was cooking)

11. I think people ___ get a good education. This is a good idea.
    (can't, won't, should, might)

12. He gives ___ homework. (a few, many, any, a lot of)

13. ___ they go to school in one more week? (did, does, will, going)

14. She is the ___ person I know. (bad, fatter, happiest, nice)

15. ___ I get up, I drink a cup of coffee. (so, before, after, then)

16. The picture is ___ the wall. (in, at, under, on)

17. Tom usually ___ until 9:00. (was sleeping, is sleeping, sleep, sleeps)

18. I'm going to buy a car, ___ I'm going to buy a television.
    (because, but, so, and)

19. Yesterday, he ___ a good movie. (seeing, sees, see, saw)

20. Last year, I ___ speak English. (won't, couldn't, mustn't, don't have to)

21. The sofa is ___ the television. (next, across from, in the corner of, on the right)

22. How many ___ of scissors do you have? (pairs, bags, pieces, cans)

23. John is ___ interesting than Bill. (as, more, not, most)

24. There are ___ bottles of glue on the table. (a little, much, a few, any)

25. You ___ get a driver's license if you drive. You have no choice. (must, can, should, might)

26. Last night, I ___ the newspaper. (am reading, read, reading, don't read)

27. The window is ___ the room. (between, at one end of, on, above)

28. It ___ now. (snowing, was snowing, snowed, is snowing)

29. In two days, I ___ on vacation. (is going to go, was going, will go, is going)

30. She ___ learn to swim, but I think she should. (mustn't, won't have to, can't, couldn't)

31. I think Paris is the ___ city in the world. (loveliest, larger, worse, expensive)

32. Jack isn't as ___ as his friends. (older, better, nice, smartest)

33. If you want to be a good tennis player, you ___ practice. (can, might, should, could)

34. How ___ sugar is there? (any, some, many, much)

35. Bill likes candy, ___ he eats a lot of it. (after, so, but, before)

B. Read the answers. Then, write the questions that go with the answers.

Examples: No, he wasn't sick yesterday.

Was he sick yesterday? _____

He takes English classes every day.

When does he take English classes? _____

1. I am reading a book.

_____

2. My husband cooked dinner last night.

_____

3. They will go to Hawaii.

_____

4. Yes, I went to the University of Michigan last term.

_____

5. The bookstore is on 12th Ave. and Main Street.

_____

6. No, I'm not having a good time.

_____

7. My sister is going to move next Saturday.

_____

8. Yes, I got my books yesterday.

_____

9. No, David isn't in New York.

_____

C. Answer the questions in complete sentences:

   Example: What did you do last night?

   (go to a party) **_I went to a party._** _____

1. What is Edward doing?

   (study) _____

2. What does Jack do every morning?

   (brush his teeth) _____

3. What will you do next week?

   (fix the car) _____

4. What does your daughter usually do after school?

   (watch T.V.) _____

5. How did you get to work?

(take the bus) _____

6. What are you doing now?

(eat breakfast) _____

7. What did you do last year?

(buy a car) _____

8. What is Tom doing?

(play soccer) _____

APPENDIX B

Irregular Verbs

simple verb	past verb	simple verb	past verb
be	was	become	became
begin	began	blow	blew
break	broke	bring	brought
build	built	buy	bought
catch	caught	choose	chose
come	came	cost	cost
do	did	draw	drew
drink	drank	drive	drove
eat	ate	fall	fell
feel	felt	fight	fought
find	found	fly	flew
forget	forgot	get	got
give	gave	go	went
grow	grew	have	had
hear	heard	hold	held
keep	kept	know	knew
lay	laid	leave	left
let	let	lose	lost
make	made	meet	met
pay	paid	put	put
quit	quit	read	read
ride	rode	run	ran
say	said	see	saw
sell	sold	send	sent
shut	shut	sing	sang
sit	sat	sleep	slept
speak	spoke	spend	spent
stand	stood	steal	stole
stick	stuck	sweep	swept
swim	swam	take	took
teach	taught	tear	tore
tell	told	think	thought
throw	threw	understand	understood
wake	woke	wear	wore
win	won	write	wrote

INDEX